From Ramen to Riches™
Building Wealth in Your 20s

Or
Spending, Saving, Investing and Managing Your Money
to Get Rich Slowly, but Surely

JAMES G. WOOD

Published by
The Tannywood Group, Inc.
San Diego, California

For updates and more resources,
please visit my website at:
www.fromramentoriches.com

Follow me on Twitter at:
www.twitter.com/fromramentorich

The author welcomes feedback to improve future editions. Due to the volume of mail he receives, the author regrets that he will be unable to respond individually to every message.

ISBN 978-0-9828251-0-5

Library of Congress Control Number: 2010934178
Library of Congress subject headings:
Finance, Personal.
Young adults — Finance, Personal.

Cover image, design, and interior formatting by Megan Condon/Incitrio.

Published by
The Tannywood Group, Inc.
San Diego, California
Contact: publishing@tannywood.com
www.tannywood.com

For Jordan

Table of Contents

Acknowledgements

It turns out that writing, publishing, and marketing a book is not such a solitary experience after all. I had heard all these stories about how authors lock themselves in an office for months on end, eating cereal three meals a day, neglecting personal hygiene, and having minimal contact with the outside world. That was not my experience at all.

When I mentioned this project to friends, I was so amazed, grateful, and humbled that so many would immediately ask how they could help. Their feedback and advice have made this book so much better than it would have otherwise been. Of course, any errors remain my responsibility alone.

My editor, Tricia Whittemore, was a huge help in tightening my prose and pointing out where something wasn't clear. Her insights were especially helpful because she is a member of my target market. (Well, at least she was when this project began!) Thanks to Megan Condon at Incitrio for the fabulous exterior cover design and interior formatting.

I am indebted to everyone who reviewed the manuscript and provided invaluable feedback: Hilary Babon, Jon Babon, Christopher Bush, Chris Christensen, Stacy Christensen, Beth Powell, Diane Rosenblum, Renée Schor, Marilyn Tanny, Jeff Whittemore, David Wood, Peter Wood, and Cindy Yang.

I am grateful to Angela Hill, AmyK Hutchens, Suzanne Livingston, Dave Smith, and Tom Jurgensen for so generously sharing their professional wisdom and advice.

Finally, to my wonderful wife Lauren, who patiently read multiple versions of the manuscript, provided insightful feedback, and introduced me to people I needed to know. Her support and faith in me inspires me to be more than I would be otherwise. I love you always and forever.

Disclaimer

I am not a financial professional. I wish I could say something cool like, "I am not a financial professional, but I play one on TV." Sadly, I haven't seen any casting calls for leading roles as an accountant or financial planner. Besides, I can't act.

I'm just a geek with a calculator who is passionate about personal finance. I started as a financially clueless 21-year-old who made many mistakes with money. I slowly learned on my own how to save, manage, and invest. Now in our 50s, my wife and I are debt free, own a house free and clear, and have built a retirement portfolio that will comfortably sustain us in the coming years.

This book is written from one consumer to another, discussing an approach to managing your money using commonly accepted rules of thumb. At times, I will offer opinions based on my experience managing my own money. You should accept or disregard those opinions as appropriate for your circumstances.

This book is for informational purposes only. The contents are not intended to be investment, legal, insurance, tax, or financial advice and should not be construed as such. I am not a financial professional and make no claims to be one. This book is not intended to replace the advice of a qualified professional, nor are the contents intended to cover every subject area available in a professional financial planning curriculum. The reader should seek the advice of a qualified professional as appropriate.

The contents of this publication are intended to help readers educate themselves about personal finance. While every effort has been made to assure accuracy as of the date of publication, there is no guarantee explicit or implied.

The contents of any third-party websites referenced in this publication are the responsibility of those parties and not the author or publisher of this book. Information about third-party websites, companies, and products is provided for the reader's convenience and does not necessarily convey a recommendation or endorsement.

Neither the author nor the publisher shall have any liability or responsibility with respect to any loss or damage caused, or alleged to be caused, directly or indirectly by the information contained in this book.

Now, let's have some fun with personal finance!

The Big Picture

"He that waits upon fortune is never sure of a dinner."
— BENJAMIN FRANKLIN

CHAPTER 1

Why This Book Matters

"You mean to tell me you've been employed as a software engineer for five years and your net worth is $500?"

Those were the first words out of the mortgage loan officer's mouth after he had finished reviewing my application. This is not what you want to hear from your banker when you're looking to borrow a large sum of money. I was 26 years old. My buddy Frank and I were sitting with the loan officer in the bank's conference room to review our joint application to buy a townhouse in the San Francisco Bay Area. (Real estate prices were so expensive in Silicon Valley that it was not uncommon for young engineers to pool their resources to buy their first property.) The banker's reaction to my financial situation was a cold jolt of reality.

It was true. Despite my great salary, I was worth a mere $500. How was that possible? After four years of college with only $30 per month to spend, when I graduated I suddenly had more money than I'd ever seen in my life. After a few years of driving old beaters, I bought a brand new Toyota Celica GT with no money down and put the tax and registration expense on my credit card. No longer wallowing in student poverty, I learned to SCUBA dive, got my private pilot's license and traveled the world. I visited Australia, New Zealand, several South Pacific islands, Mexico, Hong Kong, and a number of European countries. I put a lot of that fun on my credit card. I never missed a payment, but usually paid the minimum and went on having fun. I hardly noticed the several hundred dollars a year in credit card interest. Five years later, everything I earned had vanished.

That meeting with the mortgage banker was my epiphany. When Frank and I decided to buy the townhouse, Frank was the one who had the 20% down payment. I borrowed my 10% from him and he in turn charged me 10% interest on that cash. What I brought to the party was an income equivalent to Frank's to make the mortgage payment manageable. Together we would qualify for the loan. However, I suddenly realized that if I ever lost my job I'd be broke in two weeks, especially if I was going to take on a responsibility like a mortgage.

It felt very uncomfortable to be in such a situation. I knew that Silicon Valley's high-tech industry goes through frequent boom and bust cycles. What if I got laid off during an industry downturn? Then what? I had no spare stash of cash to rely on and was completely dependent on that twice-monthly paycheck. How could I have been so clueless about paying attention to my money? Frank had been working for about the same number of years, yet he was able to accumulate enough for a 20% down payment on a piece of property. Why hadn't I done that?

I spent the next year or two paying off Frank and getting serious about managing my money. Over the following 25 years, I successfully learned to save and invest. Now in our early 50s, my wife and I are debt free, own a house free and clear, and have built a retirement portfolio that will comfortably sustain us in the coming years. And, we've had a lot of fun along the way.

Why I Wrote This Book

The financial life I led in my early 20s is a common story in our country. We didn't discuss money much at home when I was growing up—that subject was considered a private matter. None of my classes in high school or undergraduate courses in college explained how to manage my financial life. Many of my peers shared similar experiences.

Remember the old movies where the accountant was always some dorky wimp with a pocket protector? How often were those guys the heroes? Do you think John Wayne ever played an accountant? My assertion is that we need to elevate math geeks to the realm of greater coolness. You see, in the real world, personal finance skills can mean the difference between leading a comfortable, stress-free life, or spending years drowning in debt and never having enough money to feel satisfied and happy.

Here's the best analogy I can think of. A few years back, we were visiting friends in Melbourne, Australia. People there are as crazy about a game called cricket as Americans are about football and baseball. One of my Aussie friends took me to a cricket match so that I could get a proper education in the sport. My friend patiently explained the rules over the course of the afternoon. Sadly, I left as confused as I was at the beginning. (If you think baseball is a leisurely sport, you should try cricket. Cricket matches go on for several hours a day stretched out over multiple days.) Another Australian friend commented that she didn't bother watching the sport because she thought it was "like watching paint dry."

And so it is for many people with the game of personal finance. Watching one's spending and planning for the future through investing is about as exciting for many people as it is for the uninitiated who attempt to understand cricket. The difference, however, is that you are playing the game whether you want to or not.

In every financial transaction, you are an unwitting participant in the personal money management game, be it a grocery store purchase, a night out on the town, paying the rent, or anything else. The game is going on around you all the time whether or not you want to play. It is truly the game that will have the greatest impact on your life. It's to your benefit to learn the rules and get off the sidelines. Why not play to win?

I spent many years learning this stuff, often by trial and error. I've made mistakes in my financial life, some of them expensive. I consider those mistakes to be my personal finance class "tuition money." I now have a seven-year-old son and have been thinking a lot about how I can help him avoid my early miscues as he gets older. Similarly, I have coached many friends over the years to share with them what I've learned. This book, for me, is a natural extension of that work. I'm aiming this at young adults because I'd like to help you get off to a good start in your financial life. In effect, I'd like to save you some tuition money in the arena of personal finance. As you'll see later in the book, you and your peers have one enormous financial advantage over your parents and grandparents and that is: **TIME**.

> *An investment of $4.25 per day beginning at age 20*
> *can yield a balance of more than $1,000,000 by age 70.*

The example above assumes an average 8% annual return in the stock market over the time period in question[1]. For reasons we'll discover later, the amount required to achieve that same result ($1,000,000 at age 70) gets dramatically higher the longer you wait, as follows:

- $10/day at age 30 ($300/month)—still doable, but getting more challenging;
- $23/day at age 40 ($690/month)—you will probably need a second job;
- $57/day at age 50 ($1,710/month)—so much for the vacation house;
- $186/day at age 60 ($5,580/month)—at this point, the lottery is looking better and better.

---

[1] *This is the approximate pre-tax historical long-term average stock market return, though results vary widely from year to year. We'll discuss this more in the investing section.*

What This Book Will Do (and Not Do) for You

Please understand that I am not a financial professional. Think of this book as one (somewhat older) consumer talking to another (somewhat younger) consumer. Some of the ideas that I'll share on spending, saving, and investing will resonate with you; some will not. That's fine. Use the suggestions that make sense for you—discard the others or revisit them later.

I will introduce you to many of the key concepts that are essential to personal finance, but the list will not be exhaustive or complete. I think that would be overwhelming. Additionally, the nuts and bolts of some of these subjects have been well trodden by other authors. If you'd like to take a deeper dive into some of these topics, I've included several recommended books and periodicals on my website: **www.fromramentoriches.com**.

I intend to help you understand how the game is played and get you engaged in it. I further want to challenge you to think carefully about what you're doing and whether the conventional wisdom is necessarily correct for your circumstances.

For those who are math challenged, I'll warn you that we'll be doing some work with numbers in this book. Don't worry—it won't be anything particularly complicated. I'll take care of running the numbers. Your job will be to stay with me to understand the how and why. I confess that in my first calculus class in high school, I tended to drift off to fantasies about my latest love interest rather than listening to my teacher drone on about differential equations. It wasn't until a year later in college that I finally got it. Some of the math in this book may feel like that to you. If you notice yourself drifting off to fantasyland, hang in there.

For me, financial education is a life-long pursuit. Some of the things you'll read here are enduring concepts that will serve you well for a long time. Others, like certain government tax incentives, may be obsolete by the time you read this. For this reason, I wrestled with whether to include specific numbers with things like IRA contribution limits, income tax rates, and so on. In some cases, I've referenced the figures applicable to 2010, the year this book was written. Be aware that many of these numbers change annually based on inflation rates or other formulas established by the government. Always do follow up research to see if the information still holds, if the numbers are still current, whether the government has changed the rules, or whether the eligibility limits for some particular program have changed.

I will not offer specific investment advice. However, I will attempt to explain the key things you'll need to know to make your own decisions. I will mention products or companies with which I have experience and that

I like. Some of the things that work for me may or may not be appropriate for your situation. You need to do more legwork to evaluate how to apply some of this to your life.

You, and no one else, need to take responsibility to put what you learn here into action. The last chapter will help with this. If you already have good savings and money management habits, you will have a great head start. If not, I'm sure you know that bad habits and inertia are difficult to overcome—it's like quitting smoking.

Much about what you've learned about money, good or bad, you've likely picked up from your parents, friends, and the media. Please consider the following:

- Was money tight or plentiful when you were growing up?
- Could you have anything you wanted or did you need to save up for things?
- Was there harmony or a lot of arguing at home around money?
- Did (or do) your parents bail you out of money-related problems?
- How has advertising swayed your financial decision-making?
- What role have your friends played in your spending habits?
- How do all these things affect your view of money and its role in your life?

These are not just idle questions. Your "financial philosophy" is key to how you manage many aspects of your life. We will explore this in Chapter 3.

I've informally coached many friends on how to better manage their personal finances. All have been grateful, but many have gone on doing what they've been doing and have continued to struggle with money. That's one reason why I wanted to aim this book at younger people who are just beginning to be financially independent. Most young people in this country have a realistic potential to retire as millionaires, if only they get started early and develop good habits with their money. This book will show you how to get rich slowly, but surely, and have some fun with it along the way.

Are you ready? Let's get started.

CHAPTER 2

Key Principles

As I mentioned earlier, managing your money is a game. To be an effective player at any game, you need to master the ground rules, develop effective strategies, and carefully execute the smallest of tactical details. Ignore any of these elements and you: (1) end up befuddled about what's going on around you; (2) never win the game; and (3) will not have a good time. In fact, you will likely lose interest pretty quickly, like my Australian friend who thinks watching cricket is like watching paint dry.

This chapter describes the 10 strategic principles I've developed to help play the game. In the chapters that follow, we'll cover the smaller tactical details and ground rules that you'll need to know. For now, be thinking about how the following principles might be relevant to your financial life. It's possible that not all of them will be a good fit for you. You may also think of others that are more appropriate for how you view the world. That's great! I'd encourage you to make notes as you go along to personalize and refine this list.

Principle #1: Time Is Your Ally

This is by far the most important concept in this book. If you were to take away only one thing by the time you're done reading, it would be to understand the **time value of money**. Simply put, it is better to have money now than at some point in the future because it can be invested or earn **compound interest** over time.

This is an extremely powerful concept, particularly when applied over multiple decades. It also is the greatest financial advantage that young people have over those who are older. Here are some examples to drive home the point:

1. Do you realize that if you invested $125 each month beginning at age 18 for 52 years and earned an average 8% per year in the stock market, you'd have over $1,000,000 when you reached age 70? (Actually, you would have exactly $1,166,120.) But here's the interesting thing. You would have invested only $78,000 in this scenario ($125/month x 12 months/year x 52 years) and you end up a millionaire!

---

2. If you waited until age 30 to start investing the same amount, your ending balance would drop to $436,376 at age 70. By waiting those 12 years, you lost out on $729,744!

3. Here's an interesting variation: let's say our 18-year-old in example #1 invested the $125 per month until age 40 (22 years). He or she then stopped contributing and just let the money continue to grow at the same rate of return. At age 70, the ending balance would be $979,825. This balance is more than double the result of the example #2 investor who started at age 30 and contributed for 40 years.

Our 30-year-old in example #2 had to invest $60,000. Notice that the 18-year-old in example #3 only invested $33,000, yet still ended up with $543,449 more in the bank at age 70. The additional years of compounding make a dramatic contribution to the end result.

The key thing to take away from this principle is that you must think for the very long term. Pondering retirement, for example, when that won't happen for another 40-50 years, is an extremely challenging thing to do. However, I can assure you this is an essential element of your financial success.

I am by no means suggesting that you should not spend money now to enjoy life while you are young. Far from it! What I am saying is that it should not be hard to divert a relatively small amount of money now to ensure that you can still be having fun when you're older. I am now 50 years old and am every bit as active, excited, and engaged as I was in my twenties. Planning ahead may require making some changes to your current spending habits. But I can promise you that the long-term payoff is breathtaking.

Principle #2: Avoid "Bad" Debt. Use "Good" Debt Sparingly.

One of the fastest ways to ruin your financial life is the careless use of debt. As we saw in Principle #1, compound interest works in your favor if you're a saver. It works in the same way for the bank's benefit if you're a debtor. Even worse for you, the interest rates they charge on many products can be a lot higher than you could ever possibly hope to get as a saver. For example, credit card interest can easily exceed 20% depending on your credit rating and the terms specified by the card issuer. During normal times, you would be lucky to get 5% interest on a bank savings account. (As of this writing, interest rates paid by banks on savings accounts are far lower than 5%.)

How do you distinguish between "good" debt and "bad" debt? Here's my opinion. The nominees for the **"Good" Debt** award are:

1. *Mortgage loans:* Nominated for two reasons: (1) There is a decent chance that the property you buy will appreciate over a long period of time so the money you're shelling out on interest would be at least partially recouped; and (2) Unless you're independently wealthy, it's awfully tough to pay cash for a home purchase given the dollar amounts involved. (See Chapter 8, *"Home, Sweet Home,"* for a detailed discussion on this.)

2. *Student loans:* You can generally make a good case that debt assumed for college will help you in the long run. You're likely to get a much higher-paying job with a degree than without one. Even though student loans might make sense for you, be careful. Read loan terms carefully and make sure the amount of debt you're accumulating makes sense given the average salary that people in your major tend to be offered upon graduation. If you run into trouble, student loan debt is difficult to discharge (get rid of), even in bankruptcy.

3. *A very low interest rate loan:* A loan that has a lower interest rate than the after-tax interest rate that you are earning on a risk-free[2] investment like a bank CD *might* qualify as "good" debt. For example, assume you need to buy a new car and have the cash in hand. The dealer is offering 0% financing to buy the model you want and you're getting 2% interest (after-tax) on your money at the bank. You come out ahead by taking the dealer loan in this case. (This assumes the dealer won't lower the vehicle sale price further if you pay cash instead of taking the financing offer.)

The nominees for the **"Bad" Debt** award are almost everything else, including:

1. *Credit card debt:* ESPECIALLY credit card debt. Credit cards are useful for: (1) convenience; (2) helping build a credit score (or ruin one); and (3) possibly for cash-back rebates if the issuer has established such a program. And that is all. Credit card holders who carry a balance are often paying obscene interest rates. Even worse, if you pay the minimum balance due it could take well over a decade to retire the debt. (Game score: Banker 1; Consumer 0.) Fees and interest payments to the bank could leave you in debt for a very long time.

2. *Anything used to finance "stuff":* Consumer items nearly always **depreciate** (lose value) to be worth close to nothing in fairly short order. Examples include clothes, shoes, and electronics. Have a garage sale and you'll

---

[2] *Bank deposits are currently insured by the FDIC up to $250,000 per depositor, per insured bank.*

get a good idea of the after-market value of your things. I've done it—it's not pretty. Bottom line: Always save up and pay cash for "stuff."

3. *Home equity lines of credit ("HELOCs") and 2nd/3rd mortgages:* Why would you want to increase the amount of debt owed on the roof over your head? Yet, a huge number of people did this during the real estate "bubble" years of the mid-2000s, when house prices were appreciating far beyond historical norms. Cheap credit was readily available and many people used their houses like ATM machines, with HELOCs, "cash out" refinancing and the like. Many used the extra cash to buy boats and other expensive toys or to pay for a vacation they couldn't otherwise afford. (Another game score update. Banker 2; Consumer 0.)

Similarly, some financial advisors and mortgage brokers during that period urged their clients to maximize the debt on the house and invest the extra cash in the stock market. The reasoning was, "Houses always go up in price and the stock market gives you 8-9% return on your money, which is more than you're paying on the mortgage."

Well, we know how that turned out. House prices declined nationally in the late 2000s for the first time since the Great Depression. While the stock market does tend to go up 8-9% per year on average, this number applies over a very long time horizon. The stock market actually lost money for the entire last decade. Those who followed this strategy ended up losing money on the house, on their stock market investments, AND paid a pile of wasted money to their banks and mortgage brokers. Many, in fact, lost their homes or simply walked away because the property value had declined so much they didn't see a chance of recovering the losses. Bankers and consumers both ended up losing.

Like so many other people, my family's income got hammered in the 2008-2009 recession. We felt fortunate that we had prepared ourselves by being completely debt free, including mortgage debt. Despite the reduced income, our low monthly cash flow needs and substantial cash hoard allowed us to weather the storm with a manageable level of stress. As you start your financial life, be savvy about your borrowing and strive to "pay as you go" as much as possible.

Principle #3: Distinguish Between Wants and Needs

I'll go out on a limb here and suggest that it shouldn't be too hard for most young adults to come up with the $125 per month to invest according to Principle #1. Here are some simple things my family has done that could easily generate at least that amount in savings:

- Stop drinking bottled water. We saved $35 per month. Helps the earth too!
- Stop drinking soda. We saved $60 per month for at-home and restaurant consumption.
- Switch to basic cable or delete the cable bill entirely. We use an old-fashioned antenna to pick up local TV channels and get streaming Netflix movies over the Internet, for a savings of about $50 per month.
- Reduce or eliminate fancy coffee consumption. This was a big one for me. I switched from cappuccinos five days a week to a single cup out once a week while making coffee at home the other days. Savings was $50 per month.

Do you have an expensive cell phone plan? Spend money on custom ring tones? Drink bottled water or soda? Eat junk food? Love your morning cappuccino? Drive a brand new vehicle that gets poor gas mileage? Have cable TV? Like designer clothes? Like to party at bars? I'm not saying any of these things are necessarily bad. They simply illustrate that we make choices about how we spend our money dozens of times a week.

You'll find that things you "need" to survive are pretty limited—food, shelter, insurance, transportation, and basic clothing. Everything else falls into the "want" category. Even within your basic needs, you have a lot of discretion on upgrading, which then moves some of those spending decisions back into the "want" category. For example, public transit might serve the basic need for transportation. A "want" is anything beyond that, which means you have flexibility on how you spend dollars in that area.

In the coffee, soda, and water examples shown above, I realized I could continue spending thousands of dollars on beverages that would eventually just end up in the city sewer, or I could put that money to better use. I went at this rather slowly at first because I wasn't keen on jettisoning some of the niceties to which I had become accustomed. This was particularly true of caffeine. Over time, though, I realized that my "want" list became shorter and I stopped pining for the things that added little value to my life. Similarly, disposing of things through multiple trips to various charitable agencies or via garage sales really brought home the fact that we were getting rid of a lot of stuff we didn't need in the first place. The terrific side benefit of our reduced consumption of material things is that our monthly cash flow requirements began to shrink steadily.

Now, I'm not suggesting you should deny yourself the things you really want. Avoid the binge dieter syndrome where you starve yourself by not buying anything for a while, and then go crazy with the credit card because you've denied yourself for so long. By all means, after you've honestly assessed whether a particular purchase will bring you great joy or add value to your life, go ahead and buy it if the budget allows. Just make sure the purchase is done in accordance with the next principle.

Principle #4: Never Pay Full Retail Price for Anything

With rare exception, you can get the things you want at a price much lower than the first one you come across. This is great fun. The game is based on a rather simple premise: the retailer's goal is to sell you something at the highest possible price. They're not bad people (well, most of them anyway). They're just trying to make the best profit possible and serve their customers well so they can stay in business. Your goal, once you've decided you really WANT to make a purchase, is to get the item in question for the lowest possible price. My strategies include:

- *Waiting for a big sale on non-perishable staples, then backing up the truck and buying out the store.* We have "backup stock" for a wide variety of these items. For example, I currently have about 30 boxes of our favorite cereals stored in the garage because I bought them on a big sale for a net price of $1.50 per box rather than the usual $3.99. Over the course of a year, that saves us nearly $200 on this one item alone. Multiply that by all the staples you buy and you're looking at a big bag of money. I will confess that I'm sometimes a bit too clever for my own good. My seven-year-old son was on a baked beans kick for a while. He'd consume an entire can at one sitting. When the beans went on a half-off sale, I of course bought everything on the shelf—25 cans in all. The following week the boy decided he didn't like them anymore. So Dad is now getting to rediscover the culinary joys of baked beans for himself. The good news is the cans have a three-year shelf life, which is about how long it'll take me to choke them all down.
- *Getting acquainted with the typical price of my favorite items at a variety of stores.* Sometimes one store will sell some things as a "loss leader" and make up for it by charging higher prices on other things. We're fortunate to have four major grocery chains within a few miles of our house, so we have regular shopping lists for each store based on our knowledge of where each item is cheapest.
- *Comparison shopping online.* The Internet has shifted power from retailers to consumers. It is now very easy to sit in a comfortable place, at any hour of day or night, and compare the offered prices for almost any product. The web is a great equalizer.
- *Negotiating.* Don't be afraid to negotiate, even on some of the smaller things.

I've been pretty surprised to discover that many places will do this if you are speaking with someone who has authority to make a deal. Heck, even the customer service representative of my Internet Service Provider was willing to negotiate when I told him I was thinking of switching to a competitor.

- *Reviewing expenses.* Regularly review everything you spend money on until you're sure you are getting the best price, no matter how insignificant it might seem. Remember, you're typically conducting dozens of purchase transactions every month. Shaving a little bit off every single item adds up to serious money at the end of the month.

Later in the book you'll find an entire chapter on tactics for finding the best deal on items in a variety of categories. For now, just be thinking about how you might begin to integrate this way of thinking into your spending philosophy.

Principle #5: Pay Attention

During a typical month, most of us have money leaking out of our pockets all the time. We're busy with our lives and we don't always have the time or inclination to watch every dollar of cash outflow. The spur of the moment latte, grabbing groceries on the way home from work, filling the gas tank at the nearest station—these are examples of things we might do on a hectic day. Sometimes we will trade off time for money and at times this is necessary.

Similarly, companies can make a lot of money on nuisance fees and hidden expenses if you're not paying attention. Financial services companies like banks, insurance companies, and investment management firms are particularly notorious for this. So are travel companies (airlines, hotels, rental car companies, and the like).

In most cases, fees like this can be avoided if you: (a) read the fine print; (b) compare offerings from several competitors; and (c) avoid companies that do this and give your business to those that do not.

Here's the thing: even the most trivial amount of money that leaves your pocket has a dramatic impact over the very long term. For example, I save about $5 per month on stamps by using free online bill pay or automatic payment features. You might roll your eyes and conclude that's hardly worth the effort. However, if we apply the time value of money principle, that $5 per month becomes $39,659 if invested at 8% over 50 years. That's not even factoring in the value of the time saved by doing so!

So by all means, live the life you want to live and don't feel like you need to watch every penny. Sometimes the tradeoff of time for money is worth it. All I'm saying is be aware of the consequences of multiple transactions every month where little bits of cash here and there are being unnecessarily siphoned off because you haven't been paying attention. By paying attention, you could easily be saving a lot more or be putting the money to better use for your benefit.

Principle #6: Develop Good Financial Habits Early

Have you ever had an experience where someone showed you an easier way of doing something, but you had a terrible time unlearning how you did it before?

My keenest example of that is learning how to play drums. My buddies and I formed a garage band in college. We realized we had all the instruments covered except drums. I said, "Sure, I'll do it. How hard could it be?" I bought a drum kit and spent the weekend teaching myself a drumbeat that worked. (It was the late 1970s and most of our music had the same drumbeat with minor variation.) At rehearsals and during performances, I found that I was getting extremely tired after playing for only 15 minutes or so.

Some weeks later, someone who knew what they were doing explained that the reason I was getting so tired was that I needed to hit the snare drum and the hi-hat with the opposite arms. But for the life of me, I couldn't make the adjustment and just stayed with what I'd been doing. I would get so tired by the middle of a set that I would start slowing down the tempo. My band mates would turn around saying, "Speed it up!" Needless to say, I didn't last long as a rock-and-roll drummer.

Changing ingrained habits is tough. You're much better off if you start out with good financial habits from the get-go. These habits include things like budgeting, paying credit cards in full every month, automatically saving at least 10% of your income, finding the best deals on things you want to buy, and investing money for future needs. Perhaps you have never had exposure to these topics and have been trying to figure it out on your own. If you're lucky, your parents may have instilled many of these habits in you already. Perhaps they have tried and you were in a similar space as Mark Twain in this quote:

"When I was a boy of 14, my father was so ignorant I could hardly stand to have the old man around. But when I got to be 21, I was astonished at how much he had learned in seven years."

Wherever you are starting from, your financial success will depend on your ability to identify both your good and bad habits. You'll then need to systematically root out the unhelpful habits and replace them with something that moves you closer to success. This book contains many ideas to help you. However, it will be up to you to actually put the ideas into action. The last chapter will offer suggestions on how you might approach this.

Principle #7: Understand Your Risk Tolerance

I've already shared a few examples that illustrate how to turn a relatively small amount of monthly savings into more than $1,000,000 over your working lifetime if you start early enough. You may have noticed in those examples that I assumed an 8% average annual return to get there. In normal times, you cannot get a return like that with a risk-free bank Certificate of Deposit (CD). To achieve an annual return in the 8% range you will need to be comfortable with a certain level of risk.

The stock market is one place that can possibly deliver returns like that, generally over very long time periods. You also run the risk of losing money—potentially lots of money. In fact, during the 2000s, the stock market actually lost money over that full 10-year period. That is a very long time to be waiting for a decent return. Other decades, of course, have had returns much higher, which is how you net out to an average return of 8%.

You will need to begin thinking about how much risk you are willing to take. Will you lose sleep if your hard-earned money loses even one dime in an investment? Some people do, so they end up choosing investments that are more conservative. Others are more aggressive and are willing to take bigger risks in the hopes of a better payoff over time.

There is also a subset of folks who are gamblers and treat the stock market like a casino. If you fall into this category you might as well try your luck in Vegas. There may be people who can reliably make money by day trading in stocks and following technical trends. I suspect there are very few and most of those are professionals. I am talking about prudent risk, not mindless speculation.

As a general rule, younger people can assume somewhat greater risks in their investments because they have time to make up short-term losses that the stock market or other investments may deliver. Older people tend to assume less risk because they have less time to make up any losses.

Take only the risks you are comfortable taking. Do not jeopardize your ability to sleep well. At the same time, be aware that your ability to accumulate substantial assets over a lifetime is greatly affected by your savings and investment choices.

Remember the example in Chapter 1 that demonstrated how to end up with over $1,000,000 on only $4.25 per day if invested in the stock market over 50 years? If you put the same amount of money in a super-safe bank CD earning 3% over the same period, your return drops to less than $200,000! To accumulate $1,000,000 with bank CDs at 3% you'd need to increase your monthly savings to roughly $725/month!

You are the one who must assess what you are comfortable with and what you are not. Take the time to think about it. Your risk profile may change over time. That's okay. Just be aware of it rather than going into something blindly and being shocked by a possible adverse outcome.

Principle #8: Continuously Educate Yourself

I hope this book will be a good start at introducing you to the highlights of personal finance. But, that's all it is—a start. The information I am passing on to you here was accumulated over many years of reading and trial and error. Every time I read something new, I pick up some useful tidbit that I didn't know about before. I'm also fortunate to have built a network of people who are either professionally involved in this area or have a passionate personal interest.

I'd encourage you to do the same. Subscribe to a variety of credible periodicals that cover relevant topics. Read every book you can find from well-regarded authors. My website has several suggestions. Start with those that are targeted to a mass-market audience. When those begin to feel too basic, move up to something meatier. You'll know you've hit the big leagues when you can read *The Wall Street Journal* cover-to-cover and actually understand what they're talking about.

Similarly, get to know people who are passionate about personal finance, whether as a personal hobby or who have devoted their professional lives to these topics. Find people who are both smart and have high integrity. You will learn a great deal. Sift through the information you find helpful and weigh it against related comments you've seen or heard elsewhere. You will also run into many people who have lots of opinions and talk a good game. Your challenge will be to figure out who knows what they're talking about and who does not. Don't necessarily assume that any one person's opinion is correct or complete. Do integrate the suggestions that make sense into your own approach.

Finally, understand your strengths and weaknesses and don't hesitate to ask for help when you need it. This will be especially true when you're first getting started. Even after over 25 years, I'm still learning new things as the game changes around me.

Principle #9: Know the Role You Want Money to Play In Your Life

Money is embedded into every nook and cranny of our lives. Not just physically, but philosophically. At the extremes, why do some people forsake money for a life of serving the poor and others relentlessly accumulate it even when they have more than 99% of the population? Why do some who are rich flaunt it and others live such a low-key life that their neighbors have no idea of their wealth? Why do some who aspire to the trappings of the rich subsume themselves in so much debt that in reality they are poor?

We all have some kind of philosophy about money, whether it is consciously formed or not. Our parents, our spiritual upbringing, our friends, the media, and various other sources all influence that view. Since you are still early in your independent financial life, explicitly understanding the role you want money to play in your life is an essential exercise.

What does money mean to you? How does it fit into the dreams and goals you have for your life? The next chapter on "Your Financial Philosophy and Life Vision" will help you answer those questions. Thinking about these topics proactively will enable you to frame your philosophy about money, how you want to accumulate it, and how you want to spend it.

Principle #10: This Is the Greatest Game in the World! Treat It as Such

With apologies to those few dozen of my fellow Americans who are obsessed with cricket, the game of personal finance is not like cricket! It is far from watching paint dry! I will even venture to say that it's better than basketball, baseball, football, or any other game you might find. Not that those other sports aren't great and don't have their value. In fact, if you're really good at one of them, you could potentially get paid millions of dollars to play professionally.

For the rest of us mere mortals, no other game will have such an impact on your life like mastering the rules, strategies, and tactics of managing your money. What other game can you think of that can make the average person wealthy and provide the ability to meet the material wants and needs of life?

If you're currently in the camp of "this is like watching paint dry," I hope this book will begin to change your thinking. I'm urging you in the strongest terms possible to figure out how to make this fun. Don't be a spectator oblivious to what's going on around you. I can assure you that every bank, retail store, investment management firm, and any other establishment that takes your money is playing the game with you—whether you like it or not.

You can make this a team sport if you're a social person. For example, you might consider a regular "Saving and Investment" club with like-minded friends to share ideas. If you prefer to do it on your own, create your own personal scorecard to show how much money you're saving and how your assets are growing when you begin to invest. It's very motivating to have something on paper that shows where you're achieving your "personal bests."

Think back to when you first learned a game that you're now passionate about. What was it that drew you to the game? How did you figure out the rules? What kind of practice did you need to do (and for how long) to get pretty good at it? What did it feel like to win?

These are the questions you'll need to ask yourself as you learn how to play the game of personal finance. Trust me, in several years you'll be extremely happy that you did.

CHAPTER 3

Your Financial Philosophy and Life Vision

"If you want to be happy, set a goal that commands your
thoughts, liberates your energy, and inspires your hopes."
— ANDREW CARNEGIE

Before we dive into the mechanics of personal finance, let's take a broader view to examine the role you want money to play in your life. After all, it's hard to determine how much money you'll need to live the life you want until you know what kind of life you want to live.

To accomplish this, I will request that you do two things as we make our way through this chapter. First, I will ask you to do some thinking about your philosophy about money. Second, I'm hoping to inspire you to create a "Life Vision" to explicitly articulate what you want out of your life (or at least out of the next 5-10 years). Once you have clarity on these two things, you'll be better able to develop financial goals and tactics to achieve your dreams and life vision.

Your Money Philosophy

In the last chapter, Principle #9 described the importance of developing and articulating your philosophy about money. We pondered hypothetical examples of those who are rich and flaunt it; those who are rich but you'd never know it; those who aspire to be rich but spend so much they are cash poor; and those who have no interest in material wealth whatsoever. Here is your chance to explore your views about money at a deeper level.

Find a place to think where you won't be disturbed. Please write your responses to the following[3]:

1. Consider those who have influenced your thinking about money, your values, and your purpose in life. These would likely include your parents, your spiritual advisor, your siblings, and your close friends. It could also include messages you have picked up from the media. Write down the things you've heard from all these sources that resonate with you and that you would like to carry forward in your own life. Examples

[3.] *If you are married or have a life partner, I recommend you each answer these questions separately and then discuss the answers together.*

might include things like, "Always put something aside for a rainy day." Or, "It's important to give to those who are less fortunate than ourselves."

2. Do the same for messages you have picked up from these sources that do not resonate and you would like to cast off.

3. Do you aspire to achieve tremendous wealth or is money simply an enabler for a comfortable lifestyle? Perhaps there is something in between? What feels right for you?

4. How important are material possessions in your life? Do you like having designer clothes, a fancy car, a big house, etc.? Be honest with yourself. What are your values about "stuff" as compared with obtaining more education or funding life experiences like travel, etc.? In what areas will you choose to spend your money?

5. How important is financial freedom for you? Do you like the idea of being able to walk away from a job you don't like because you have no debt and sufficient savings in the bank to sustain you? Could you perhaps back off a bit on your savings goals because you know for certain you want to work continuously until age 70? Or do you want to save aggressively so that you can be free of working for others when you are in your forties?

6. Are you easily able to defer gratification from obtaining material possessions or do you want to buy right away regardless of the financial impact? How much does peer pressure and advertising influence your spending decisions?

7. How important is it that your close acquaintances (particularly your spouse or life partner) have similar views about money as you?

8. How does "sharing the wealth" with others fit into your views about money?

9. Do you actively engage in managing the financial aspects of your life or do you prefer to delegate that to someone else?

10. If you won $10 million in the lottery, what would you do with it?

Consider your responses to the ten questions above. Using those answers to guide you, answer the following question: "What role do I want money to play in my life?" Your answer should be concise, probably no more than a paragraph. Think of it as an "elevator speech" where you're riding down to the lobby with someone and you have about 20 seconds to recite your answer.

To give you an example, here is my elevator speech to answer that question:

> "The primary value of having money is that
> it buys me freedom to live my life as I want. It also
> allows me to support my family and share it with
> those less fortunate. Finally, a healthy bank account allows
> us to splurge on travel, adventure, and good food."

Your answer may look entirely different. That's okay! The key point is that you should be able to clearly articulate the "meaning of money" for your life. The answer ends up driving many of the decisions you will make, so it is to your benefit to have consciously thought about it.

Now that you've articulated the role you want money to play, you will want to use that as one of your inputs into the development of a Life Vision.

Your Life Vision

A Life Vision is a written description of what you'd like your life to look like five or more years in the future. A vision statement is an inspiring and compelling narrative that paints a picture of your life when your goals and dreams have been fulfilled and you're living in a way that's consistent with your values. It is written in the present tense, as though it has already unfolded the way you'd like. Think of it as an ongoing inspiration for living your life and for going after your dreams. It will also help focus your actions as you think about making big life plans and decisions.

As an example, here is the vision that my wife Lauren and I crafted in the year 2000:

Our Lives Together

"We wake up each morning with the love we feel for each other, our friends, our family, and everyone in our lives. We are the proud parents of a beautiful child who is growing up to be a wonderful human being. We cherish our friends and family and actively include them and their contributions in our lives.

The company we've created is making a powerful difference in the lives of the people we serve by helping them realize their dreams. Our contributions center on empowering people and bringing them joy. We conduct ourselves with integrity, our work feels like play, and everyone we work with loves their job more than anything they've ever done.

Our frequent travels around the world are filled with adventure, fun, and romance. And when we return to San Francisco, we're inspired each day with its energy, diversity, food, and beauty. We're lucky to live here.

At the end of each day as we fall asleep in each other's arms, we're grateful for each other and our child, for our health, and for what we have and what we give. We can't wait for tomorrow!"

We framed the finished product and hung it on a wall where we can easily see it. At the time we wrote it, we were childless and seemed to have little possibility of being parents because Lauren was 44 years old. Well, two years later Lauren gave birth to our now seven-year-old son.

Similarly, we had both been working for a corporate paycheck for a couple of decades, and the dream of running our own company had barely occurred to us prior to sitting back and thinking about what we really wanted. Lauren now runs her own consulting company that helps people realize their dreams and become more successful leaders. I run the back office part-time. Finally, this book itself is the direct result of some of the thinking in our vision: "... making a powerful difference ... by helping people realize their dreams. Our contributions center on empowering people and bringing them joy."

My purpose in sharing our vision statement is twofold. First, it gives you an example to look at. Second, it helps demonstrate how to create a linkage between your Life Vision and your personal finances. The vision, in fact, informs the monetary requirements that you'll need in order to achieve the vision.

Take another look at the vision that Lauren and I created. Notice that it doesn't explicitly talk about money. However, you can get some good clues by reading carefully: "proud parents of a child ... frequent travels around the world ... and when we return to San Francisco ...". Anyone who has left their heart in San Francisco also leaves copious quantities of cash there as well! It's an extremely expensive place to live. "Frequent travels around the world"—that one's pretty obvious. "Having a child"—for those of you who haven't crossed this threshold yet, I can say that being a parent is a great joy despite the occasional challenges. And, supporting children requires a pretty good bank balance or paycheck.

Here are a couple of hypothetical abbreviated vision statements to consider:

> "Regularly fly on my personal jet from Palm Beach to hang out with my investment banker friends in New York ... visit each of my five vacation homes at least quarterly ..."

> "Commune with nature in the woods of Oregon in the log cabin I've built myself. Eat sustainable foods that I've grown in my own organic garden ..."

Pretty clear which one will require significant chunks of cash to realize, huh? This is how your vision will help inform your financial goals.

To get started writing your vision, find a place that inspires you, where you can think big about your life. Perhaps at the ocean, a lakefront, or a mountaintop. Maybe you'll choose a place with a beautiful view that has always moved you. Pick any place that has significant meaning to you. Allow your mind to dream, to think big. At times, your brain might say, "That's impossible." Ignore it. If it persists, perhaps this Mark Twain quote will help:

> *"Twenty years from now you will be more disappointed
> by the things that you didn't do than by the ones you did do.
> So throw off the bowlines. Catch the trade winds in your sails.
> Explore. Dream. Discover."*

Jot down everything that comes to mind that excites you, that moves you, that inspires you. Don't worry about getting the wording right. You can do that later. Get everything out of your brain and onto the paper.

By the way, if you have a partner this is a great exercise to do together. It will help the two of you gain some clarity around how you'd like your "life together" to unfold. Lauren and I found that developing a Life Vision forced us to think about things like:

- If we have a child will one of us quit our corporate job?
- If we start a business how will we fund it?
- If we want to travel frequently in retirement, how big must the bank account be by then?
- How do we want to give back to the community and the world?

As you think about your Life Vision, you can be as specific or vague as you like. It's perfectly fine to include a specific reference to your financial situation if that is relevant for you. For example, you could say something like, "Accumulate $2 million by the time I'm 40 to give me financial freedom and allow me to give back to the community."

Here are some things you might consider as you're thinking about your vision:

- What are you passionate about?
- What dreams did you have as a kid (or still have) that you'd love to accomplish if there were no constraints on you?
- What are your values?
- Do you want to own a house?
- What unmet educational goals do you have?

- What do you want out of life in the next several years? If it doesn't strain your brain too much, think even longer term.
- Do you have or want to have children? Will you or your partner stay at home with them? Will they go to public school or private school? How will their college educations be funded?
- What do you want others to say about your life?

Visit your special place (or places) as many times as you'd like until the ideas stop coming. Then, gather the ideas into a coherent document that describes where you want to go with your life in the next 10 years. Write it in present tense, as if it is already here. You'll know you're done when you and everyone you share it with is inspired and excited by what they read. Type it up on fancy paper, frame it, and hang it on a wall where you can look at it often. Read it whenever you need inspiration. It need not be a static document. Feel free to change it as your life circumstances evolve or when new inspirations show up for you.

At this point, you have an inspiring document hanging on the wall containing a vision that likely has several components. Money (or lack thereof) will influence some of these things. Other parts of the vision will not be relevant at all to your financial situation.

Your next step will be to think about how to turn the vision into reality. There's a Japanese proverb that says, "Vision without action is a daydream. Action without vision is a nightmare." Once you have the vision complete, you'll likely avoid the nightmare part of the proverb. Now, the trick is to keep this work from becoming just a daydream.

Your vision was written to describe what you'd like your life to look like five to ten years into the future. Obviously you won't achieve everything in the next 90 days or even the next few years. What you can begin to think about, however, is a rough timeframe for how you want to organize your goals so that you can see how each might fit together holistically.

One way to start this planning process is to develop a matrix that looks something like this (for a hypothetical 22-year-old):

My Life Goals And Dreams	Next 90 Days	2 Years	5 Years	10 Years
My Relationships			Get Married	Have A Child
My Work	Get A Job!	Get Promoted	Move Into Management	Start A Company
My Adventures		SCUBA In Australia	Learn To Fly	
Things I Want To Learn		Learn To Paint	Finish M.S. Degree	
Where I Live	Find An Apartment		Buy A House	
My Financial Goals	Start Savings Plan	Emergency Fund Complete	House Down Payment	$100K Net Worth
Giving Back	Volunteer At Non-Profit	Develop Giving Plan		Help At Kid's School

The items I've placed in the cells above are obviously just examples. You get the idea. If you are a planner like me and like this approach, you can put a lot more detail into each cell, making sure that everything in your vision gets mapped into it somewhere. Feel free to include multiple items in a cell if necessary. If you are not a planner, at least do an overview framework (like the above) to give you perspective.

You can even go a step further and do some research to attach specific monetary numbers to items in cells that will require cash to implement. Examples might include the cost of college education for your master's degree, the amount you would need for a house purchase down payment, and so on. As you make your way through this book you should become better equipped to make cost assessments for the goals that require cash to make it happen. Chapter 13 (*"Your Magic Number"*) has more specifics on setting and achieving longer-term financial goals.

Filling in the Details

For each item from your Life Vision that you have placed into one of the boxes on this matrix, I would next encourage you to develop a plan that works back into the steps required to make it happen.

As an example, let's work with the "Emergency Fund Complete" box that is listed under the "2 year" goals column. We'll assume your expenses are $1,500 per month. You have an initial goal to build a three-month emergency fund. That way, if you lose your job or have an unexpected large expense, you have a cushion of cash to rely on in your hour of need.

Since this one is a short-term financial goal, it is fairly straightforward to compute the dollar amount required. Simply multiply the $1,500 by 3 months and you arrive at $4,500—this would be the amount required to fund your emergency account.

Next you would need to arrive at a monthly savings goal to get to this number. The easiest approach is to simply divide $4,500 by 24 months. (Remember, you wanted to have the emergency account funded in two years— 24 months.) The result is approximately $180 per month that you would need to save. (I rounded down a bit to account for interest that you would earn from the bank.) For long-term financial goals, you will need the help of a financial calculator to determine the correct answer. Remember that the power of compound interest over long periods greatly reduces the amounts you need to save. See Chapter 13 (*"Your Magic Number"*) for more detailed discussions on long-term money goals and financial calculators.

If you are already saving the required $180 per month, then you might be done detailing the actions needed to achieve this goal. If not, you might need to add additional steps. These steps would likely include a specific list of expenses that you will cut to raise your savings to the required amount.

You would want to repeat the process for each of the boxes in your matrix. Working backwards to the present, the result is a specific set of actions that would set you on your way to achieving your goals and dreams. Obviously, it is easier to work through the steps required for goals that are only a year or two into the future than it might be for items that are very long term. That's okay, because once or twice a year, you can go through the same process to update and refine the items on your list.

If you are not a planner and/or the idea of a matrix doesn't resonate, fair enough. (I can hear you now: "How can I possibly know that I'll get married in five years?") The point is that you will need to devise some mechanism that works for you to ensure that the vision and your dreams don't just hang on the wall like a piece of art and never become real for you.

A final suggestion: one of the best ways to improve the odds that you will get some forward momentum on this is to choose three things that you'd like to do now to move your vision forward. Then, tell three people what these things are and by when you want to have them accomplished. Ask them to check in with you to hold you accountable for getting these tasks done. If you know that three people whom you value highly are going to ask you about whether you met your commitment, you're much more likely to swing into action than you would be otherwise.

Covering the Basics

> *"That which we persist in doing becomes easier. Not that the nature of the task has changed, but our ability to do so has increased."*
> — RALPH WALDO EMERSON

CHAPTER 4

Getting Started

"Banking establishments are more dangerous than standing armies."
— THOMAS JEFFERSON

The contents of this chapter assume you are just beginning your independent financial life. Perhaps you're in college or starting your first full-time job. For you grizzled veterans of the work force, I'd encourage you to at least skim this section, as I hope you will pick up a few nuggets of useful information as well. Many other authors have covered these topics in depth, so my intent here is to give an overview of the key items that you need to understand. If you'd like more exhaustive coverage of these (and other) nuts-and-bolts introductory topics, I have included several recommended books and other resources on my website.

Getting a Checking Account, Debit Card, and Credit Card

One of the first things you'll need to take care of, if you haven't already done so, is to get a checking account paired with a debit card for withdrawals. A debit card is similar to a credit card, except the money is removed from your account immediately.

The trick is to find an account that does not have any of the sneaky fees that banks, especially big ones, like to charge you. I'm talking about monthly service charges, ATM fees, minimum balance fees, and so on.

I'm sure you've seen all the ads from "Behemoth Bank" about how you're a part of their big happy family, right? Forget all that. The business on the other side of the table is trying to extract as much money as they can. Your goal is to get what you want and pay as little as possible. Banks are very good at playing this game. You need to outsmart them.

If you are paying $12.50 per month for the privilege of letting the bank hold your money, that is 10% of the $125 per month you need to save for 50 years to become a millionaire. If you're in this unhappy situation, find another institution that won't charge the fee and you will have a good start toward the savings plan we'll discuss later.

I am personally a big fan of credit unions. These financial institutions are not-for-profit and are owned by their members. Since they are not profit-seeking entities, they can pass the savings along to members in the form of higher deposit rates and lower loan rates. They exist to serve their members (truly) and in my experience are much less likely to be perpetrators of the fee game. I pay no annoying fees on my credit union checking account and they pay me a pretty good interest rate on my savings. They have a good network of ATMs. I have also obtained most of my home mortgages with the same credit union. I have not had an account at a mega-bank in many years.

How safe is your money at a credit union? Well, the National Credit Union Administration (NCUA) is the independent federal agency that supervises federally chartered credit unions. NCUA operates a depository insurance fund similar to the insurance fund the FDIC operates for banks. For more information about credit unions and for details on how to find one in your area, visit the NCUA website (**www.ncua.gov**). If you can't find a local credit union that you're eligible to join or if you would rather search for a bank that has low-cost offerings, you could go to Bankrate.com™ to help you locate one that meets your needs. Bankrate.com™ also has a service that rates the financial strength of the credit union or bank that you are considering.

You will probably also want to get a credit card, as it can be a challenge to operate in our electronic society without one. But before I go any further, let me repeat what I said in Chapter 2 ("*Key Principles*"). Credit cards are useful for: (1) convenience; (2) helping build a credit score (or ruin one); and (3) possibly for cash-back rebates if the issuer has established such a program. And that is all. If you cannot reliably pay off your card in full each month, switch to a cash payment system until you get your spending under control.

At a minimum, your credit card should have no annual fee. Ideally, it will also offer a cash rebate feature. How nice! More free money! If you charge $1,200 per month to a card with a 1% cash rebate, that's another 10% ($12) of the money you need to save each month to become a millionaire in 50 years. See how easy saving can be once you pay attention to the little stuff?

Costco® members can currently obtain a no-fee American Express® card that rebates between 1-3% of your money, depending on the type of purchase. You can search on Bankrate.com™ for similar offerings. Again, read the fine print. Sometimes a bank will tease you with a "cash back" offering, and then burden the card with a variety of fees that cancel out the cash rebate benefits.

Understanding Your Credit Score

Your credit score underpins many things in the financial world. Examples of when your credit score comes into play include: applying for a credit card, signing an apartment lease, taking out a loan, and increasingly, when you are applying for a job.

Why does this matter? Well, a landlord will not be eager to rent to you if you have a lousy credit score because he or she will be concerned about your dependability in paying the rent every month. An employer might check your credit report and be reluctant to hire you because they might figure that if you're a deadbeat in managing your finances, you're unlikely to ever become "Employee of the Month." With loans or credit cards, a good credit score can mean a much better interest rate because the lender believes there's a good chance they'll get their money back.

A low credit score may mean much higher interest rates because you're a higher risk. Even worse, if you have a bad credit score, your loan application may be denied entirely.

The most commonly used credit scoring model is one developed by Fair Isaac Corporation, which is why you often hear this number referred to as your FICO® score. Components of the score include the following, listed in descending order of importance[4]:

- Payment history (Do you pay your bills on time?)
- Amounts owed (dollar amount and percentage of available credit used)
- Length of credit history (length of time you've had credit)
- New credit (number of applications for additional credit over a certain period of time)
- Types of credit in use (for example, "revolving debt" like credit cards and "installment debt" like student loans and mortgages)

Key inputs to the credit score calculation are data compiled in your credit files by the major credit reporting agencies: Experian, TransUnion, and Equifax. These companies collect all kinds of information relevant to your use of credit. By law, you are entitled to see your credit report for free once per year. (Visit **www.annualcreditreport.com**.) It's a good idea to do this because:

1. Credit files sometimes contain inaccurate information. You have the right to challenge inaccurate entries in your file.
2. By glancing at your credit report, you can see if someone has stolen your financial identity and is opening fraudulent accounts in your name. (This is called "identity theft." More on this below.)

The free annual credit report does not include your credit/FICO score. You'll have to pay extra to get that. There are a number of "free credit report" scams out there. Be careful that you are visiting a legitimate site.

---

[4] *Information about FICO and credit scoring is provided by Fair Isaac Corporation, and is used with permission. Copyright © 2001-2010 Fair Isaac Corporation. All rights reserved. Further use, reproduction, or distribution is governed by the FICO Copyright Usage Requirements, which can be found at www.fico.com.*

For more information about credit scores and credit reporting, visit **www.myfico.com/crediteducation**. The bottom line: your credit score and credit reports are extremely important to your financial life. Nurture them. Pay your bills on time. Avoid carrying high credit balances and pay in full each month! Use credit responsibly.

Identity Theft

Identity theft is when someone uses your personal information to commit theft and fraud. This is a serious problem and can be pretty nasty to resolve if you become a victim. The thief might open credit cards or take out loans in your name, charge purchases to a legitimate credit card that you own, file for medical or other benefits by using your Social Security number, and so on. To reduce the odds of this happening, you should:

- Keep your Social Security card in a safe place at home or in a bank vault, not in your wallet. Don't put your Social Security number on any documents unless absolutely necessary.
- Review your credit report annually (see above).
- Shred bank statements, credit card statements, and other similar paper documents when you no longer need them.
- Convert to online statements rather than paper statements so that thieves cannot steal this information from your mailbox.
- Online security: Choose secure passwords for your online accounts and change them periodically. Carefully guard all passwords and PINs. Use different passwords for each financial account. Avoid using public computers to access your online accounts that contain sensitive data. Install anti-virus software on your computer.

The government's Federal Trade Commission has a website devoted to this topic at **www.ftc.gov/bcp/edu/microsites/idtheft**.

Budgeting

Ah, budgeting. I will confess right now that this is one of my financial character flaws. I've never had the patience for dealing with budgeting details "by the book." Let me explain how it is supposed to work. Then, I'll tell you what I do for myself.

Find a piece of paper or start a spreadsheet. Think of all the major expense categories that you have. Then create a table that looks something like this:

Category	Budgeted Amount	Actual Expense	Difference
Savings			
Housing			
Utilities			
Transportation			
Clothing			
Entertainment			
Etc.			
Total			

You can build the spreadsheet to do this for one month or for the entire year.

At month end, add up all your receipts for each category (including any cash out of pocket) to determine whether you were under or over budget. This allows you to make appropriate adjustments for the next month so that you do not overspend.

This method is fairly low-tech but can be rather time consuming. Here's an even simpler approach. It assumes you spend only cash and do not use credit or debit cards. (Honestly, this method might be preferred if you never seem to have enough money at the end of the month or continually carry a balance on your credit card.) Use the same categories you created above. Cash your paycheck and place the appropriate (budgeted) amounts of money into an envelope labeled for that category. Fixed expenses, like the rent payment, get funded first. Optional items like entertainment get funded last. When there is no more money in the envelope for that expense category, you know you're done for the month.

Let's move on to more high-tech approaches. Quicken® is one of the grand-daddies of personal money management software. I have a couple of brothers who are Quicken® fanatics and swear by it. There are other software packages out there that do similar things. Quicken® allows you to automatically import data from your bank, credit card company, broker, etc. to simplify the process of tracking your expenses and determining how they compare with your budget. Another newer high-tech option you might want to research is Mint.com

---

(www.mint.com), which is owned by Intuit®, the providers of Quicken®. It's a free online service that can perform many of the same functions.

Please note that I have no personal experience with any of these online services or personal finance software and am not recommending or endorsing any of them. I am personally skittish about releasing any of my bank account information to any company, regardless of how good their security is purported to be. I tend to be rather old school on that sort of thing. You might be more comfortable with this. Do your own research and decide if one of these products might help you and whether the security and privacy safeguards meet your standards.

So, if I don't use any money management software or online service, how do I handle my budgeting? I'm sure any financial professional reading this will cringe. Since I already admitted my character flaw, here goes. It's very simple, really. My six-month "emergency fund" (see below) is fully funded and is stashed at my credit union earning decent interest in our checking account. All I do is check my starting and ending checking account balance every month. As long as the ending balance is greater than the starting balance, I'm a happy guy. If not, I've got work to do to figure out what happened. On rare occasions, the emergency fund provides a cushion if I get an unexpected surprise. When that happens, I work to replace that cash ASAP.

There are two reasons why this works. First, my wife and I are relentless about eliminating unnecessary expenses and finding ways to pay the least amount of money on everything else. Chapter 6 ("*Spending*") goes into great detail on how you might manage your spending in the same way. It's a great game! Second, we have an emergency fund to draw upon if necessary. (If you don't have a lot of savings and are working to pay down debt, I would not recommend managing your budget this way.)

So, pick one of these approaches or design one that works for you. The important thing is that you pay attention to what is going on with your cash flow every month! Keep an eye on your checking account. (Since you are paying off your credit card in full every month, we don't have to worry about that, right?) If you don't end up with more money at the end of the month than you did when you started, that's an indicator that more is flowing out than in. That's not good. Even Uncle Sam has been spending a lot more than he takes in for the last several years, but he gets to print the money! Eventually, he'll be in trouble too if that doesn't stop. Chapter 6 ("*Spending*") won't help Uncle Sam with his spending problem, but it will help you.

Start Saving! Build an Emergency Fund

The first few years of my professional life I lived paycheck to paycheck and had no cash cushion. I wasn't paying attention and instead chose to spend everything on fun and "stuff." I was lucky. If I had been laid off or had an unexpected expense (think medical emergency, major car repair, etc.), I would have been in deep trouble pretty quickly. Don't take the chance that I took.

As soon as you get your first paycheck, I recommend that you start building a savings account that eventually will have enough money in it to cover your expenses for three to six months. The easiest way to do this is to set up an account that will automatically transfer at least 10% of your paycheck directly to the bank so that you never see it. (Some people call this, "Paying yourself first.") Since this money will be earmarked for financial emergencies, you will want to put it in an account where you can get to it quickly with little or no penalty. Try Bankrate.com™ to find the best savings rates available both locally and nationally.

If money is tight and 10% is initially too much, then start with something! Use the ideas in Chapter 6 ("*Spending*") to free up cash and divert some of the savings to this account.

Whenever you get a raise at work, change your automatic savings transfer to put at least half of the new money into the bank. The key is to make sure the money goes directly to savings so that you never see it. Once you get used to having the money it is easy to permanently increase your spending. Be careful to avoid this trap.

Once you have fully funded your emergency account with money to cover three to six months of living expenses, by all means continue the savings regimen! Once you get to that point, you will be ready to start thinking about investing your additional savings for the long term. The investing chapters later on will cover this in detail.

Insurance

There are a great many risks in life. Insurance companies sprouted a long time ago to help consumers manage that risk. Insurance products can save your financial life, or in the case of health care insurance, your physical life if you are seriously injured. The trick is sorting out what insurance you need and how much. I think it would be crazy to go without some types of insurance. Other types of policies are optional, depending on the risks you are willing to assume yourself.

Automobile Insurance

In all states that I know of, you are required to carry automobile liability insurance if you drive a vehicle. If you're under 25 and especially if you're a guy, you've probably discovered by now why your parents were griping about how much their auto insurance bill went up when they added you to the policy. It's expensive to buy auto insurance when you are young. If you drive a high-performance car or have a poor driving record, the expense can be shocking! Still, you must carry a policy to be legal.

Liability insurance covers payments to others if you injure them or damage their property when you are at fault in an accident. The minimum coverage limits in many states are often quite low and may be insufficient to cover your liability if you are sued. Since you will be accruing lots of financial assets after reading this book, the last thing you want is to lose those assets in a lawsuit because you didn't carry sufficient insurance. Consult with a good insurance agent to get recommendations on limits of coverage that would be sufficient for you.

Liability coverage is only one component of a good auto policy. **Uninsured** or **underinsured motorist** coverage is often recommended to protect you if someone who isn't insured or is inadequately insured injures you or damages your property. If you are driving a relatively new vehicle, you will also want to get **collision** and **comprehensive** coverage. In fact, if you are financing or leasing the vehicle, the lender will require you to have this. Collision coverage pays for damage to your vehicle if you are at fault in an accident. Comprehensive covers damage resulting from theft, fire, and other incidents not considered a "collision."

The collision and comprehensive components of your policy are subject to certain **deductibles**. A deductible is the amount that you are responsible for before the insurance company makes its contribution. So, if you have a $2,000 loss and a $500 deductible, you pay the first $500 and the insurance company pays $1,500. If you are willing to accept a bit more financial risk, you could consider increasing your deductible in exchange for a lower premium. (Of course, this strategy might be wise only if you have made good progress building your emergency fund.)

Most insurance companies also offer add-on coverage like roadside assistance, medical payments to others, loss of use, and so on. Again, please consult with a good insurance agent who can explain what is available and what they recommend for your situation. Actually, here's a better idea: talk to three or four agents and try some online services to see if you get similar recommendations and quotes. You will likely find quite a range of price quotes for similar coverage. Like any other purchase, shopping around makes you a better consumer. And, as you'll see in Chapter 6 ("*Spending*"), comparison shopping often puts a good chunk of cash back in your pocket.

Chapter 7 ("*Automobiles*") is devoted exclusively to cars. Read it and find out why driving a sturdy eight-year-old boring sedan can put literally hundreds of thousands of dollars back in your pocket over a driving lifetime when compared with frequently leasing the latest cool "must-have" set of wheels. Insurance savings are only one part of the equation.

Renters or Homeowners Insurance

When you are just starting out, you will likely be renting an apartment or a room in a house. In this case, it would be wise to take out a renters insurance policy to cover damage or loss to your personal property. If your only possessions are a couple pairs of jeans and your furniture is mostly just milk crates, then this will be quite inexpensive. Your landlord's policy will not cover your stuff. Also, many policies give you some liability protection in the event someone gets injured at your place.

If you own a home and have a mortgage, your lender will require you to buy a policy that covers damage to the property and its contents that results from fire and other perils. Obviously, if you don't have a mortgage but own a house, you'll want this coverage to protect your investment.

It might be to your benefit to bundle your policies with one company to get discounts on multiple policies. For example, most companies that offer auto insurance also offer renters coverage. As always, you should comparison shop with multiple insurers. Chapter 6 ("*Spending*") has ideas to help.

"Umbrella" Liability Insurance

No, this won't protect you if you get caught in the rain with a leaky bumbershoot. Think of it as a policy that floats over the other liability coverage that you have with your auto and homeowners/renters policies. These are fairly inexpensive policies typically sold in increments of $1,000,000 that provide coverage over and above that provided by the policies underneath it. As your wealth builds, this type of policy will become more important. Consult with your insurance agent to determine whether this coverage would be advisable for you.

Health Care Insurance

If you are lucky, your employer provides this coverage and you don't have to worry about it. Increasingly, many employer policies share costs with employees. Employees' costs will vary by type of coverage. Carefully review the documents your employer provides and don't hesitate to ask someone in the Employee Benefits department if you have any questions.

Millions of people are not so lucky. Their employer may not offer health care insurance or they may be unemployed. If you are in this situation, you may be eligible to continue coverage under your parents' policy depending on your age and situation—be sure to check on this.

Buying a policy in the individual market can get expensive as you age. For younger people in good health, the price is often much more reasonable. In my opinion, you do not want to go without health insurance. A single accident, even something relatively minor, can result in shockingly high medical bills. In fact, a significant portion of all bankruptcies in the United States is the result of medical bills.

Don't let this happen to you. If you don't have employer-provided coverage and cannot be covered under your parents' plan, see Chapter 6 ("*Spending*") for ideas on shopping for policies.

Other Insurance

Depending on your situation, you might want to consider other types of insurance. A **disability insurance** policy will replace a portion of your income if you are no longer able to work due to a disability. What would you do if you were seriously injured in an accident and couldn't work for several weeks or months? How would you pay your bills? A disability policy could significantly relieve the financial stress.

Term life insurance pays your beneficiaries if you die. This is important coverage if you have dependents. The cost for a young, healthy non-smoking person is usually pretty low.

You may also hear about "**whole life insurance**" which is life insurance paired with a retirement savings plan. Be careful with these policies. Often, they come loaded with high fees and commissions for the agent and are not necessarily a good deal for the consumer. As you will see in the next chapter on Uncle Sam, there are many low-cost, tax-efficient retirement plans that are good vehicles for retirement savings. Whole life insurance policies don't generally fall in this category, in my opinion. A whole life policy may be appropriate for some people in special circumstances. I'm just suggesting you approach them with caution.

Dental insurance, obviously, covers care of your teeth. If your employer does not provide coverage, you could consider buying an individual policy. Alternatively, you could crunch the numbers to determine whether to self fund your dental work. If you are healthy and have a history of only requiring routine dental care, then taking a chance on paying out of pocket might make sense for a while. Find out how much an individual policy costs, and then ask your dentist for cost information on procedures you will likely need. Do the math, assess your emergency fund status, and decide how much financial risk you are willing to assume.

Many employers, especially large companies, provide coverage for medical, dental, vision, life, and disability. Be sure to read through the materials carefully to understand the coverage your employer already offers, then decide whether you need to supplement with an individual policy that you buy on your own.

With all your insurance products, you need to review the coverage you have from time to time. As your assets grow and your life becomes more financially complicated, your insurance needs will change as well. Be sure to increase coverage when you have more to protect.

What If You Already Accumulated a Lot of Debt Before Reading This Book?

You probably remember from the beginning of the book that I was in poor financial shape in my early 20s, despite having a well-paying job. I had a big chunk of credit card debt and had no savings. So, I can empathize. However, I will warn you that I am now like a reformed, ruthless ex-smoker who incessantly hounds his former smoking buddies to quit.

For those just finishing college, you are not alone if you have many thousands of dollars of student loans and credit card debt hanging over you. My experience suggests that it will take at least two or three years to dispose of the high-interest debt once you get serious about dealing with it. It may take much longer.

What do I suggest you do if you are in debt and are having a hard time getting rid of it? Here are some ideas:
- Stop using the credit card and pay cash for everything.
- Get a cheaper apartment, get roommates, or move in with your parents.
- Sell your car and walk, bike, or use public transit instead. Insurance, gas, repair expenses will also plummet.
- Stop drinking soda, bottled water, fancy coffee, and any other beverage that requires cash. Drink tap water instead.

- Stop eating out at restaurants. Picnic at the park instead.
- If your underwear and socks wear out, then fine, replace them. Otherwise, don't buy any new clothing and shoes until you are out of debt—last season's apparel will function just fine.
- Find entertainment options that are free.
- Drop cable TV and use an antenna.
- Cancel your cell phone when the contract is up and use an inexpensive pre-paid cell phone service instead.

Relentlessly scrutinize all expenses and delete everything that is optional and figure out how to obtain the essentials at a discount. Are you getting the idea?

For those of you in debt who have done all of the above and cash flow still isn't working out: wow, I don't envy your position at all. However, I do know this. If you have the discipline to manage your expenses as I described, you have the fortitude to fix the other side of the equation—your income. You might consider going back to school to upgrade your skills to get a better paying job. Perhaps you could take on a second job for a while until you've tackled the debt. Whatever you do, have confidence that you can fix it. Anyone who can manage their expenses down to just the essentials clearly has the smarts and guts to take on boosting income to a satisfactory level.

For the rest of you debt-ridden consumers, it's all under your control. No one else spent that money in the first place so no one else is going to be able to get it under control but you. No excuses. You can do this! You just need to get in gear and make it happen. The chapters that follow on spending have more ideas to help you.

As you start managing expenses better and spare cash becomes available, you should pay off your highest interest rate debt first. This is typically credit card debt. Look at your statements to determine for sure. If your experience is like mine, it will take a while but will be immensely gratifying when you succeed. Then you can be a reformed over-spender like me and hound all your indebted friends to get on the wagon. Seriously, if you are finding that you cannot control impulse spending, you might also consider talking with a therapist or finding a debtor's support group to help you.

The Stuff You Don't Want to Think About, But Should

You're young and healthy. Life is great. There's no need to start planning for your untimely demise for a number of years yet, right?

Well, not so fast. Bad things sometimes happen. I wish you a wonderful and healthy life into your 90s and beyond. Just in case, though, you should take care of some paperwork that will communicate your wishes if you are incapacitated or unexpectedly go to the great party city in the sky.

Whether you choose to deal with this now or in a couple of years, it is something you will need to take care of at some point. Some of these documents become even more important when you have dependents (spouse and/or kids) and when you have accumulated significant assets.

In the event you become incapacitated, there are various legal documents that allow you to specify your wishes for medical treatment and to identify someone you trust to make medical decisions on your behalf. The laws and document titles vary a bit from state to state. Some of the document names you might hear include a **durable power of attorney for health care, living will**, and **advance directive**. Your state may have some variation on how the contents are structured and described. Your health care provider may be able to give you the proper form to specify your preferences for medical treatment or you may want to consult with an attorney to draft the appropriate documents. The key point is that you should document in advance how you want your medical care to proceed if you are incapacitated and who should make decisions on your behalf.

While you're with your attorney, he or she will also likely suggest a couple other things. One is a **durable power of attorney**, which enables you to specify who you want to act on your behalf for legal, business, and/or financial matters if you are unable to do so yourself.

Your attorney will also want you to draft a **last will and testament** to specify who you want to manage the disposition of your estate and how to distribute your assets after you're gone. If you have a more complex financial and life situation, the attorney may also suggest creating a **revocable living trust** and other estate planning documents.

You will want to review and possibly revise the above documents when you have a major life event, like a marriage, divorce, or the birth of a child.

For more education on these topics, try **www.nolo.com** and other consumer legal education websites. Then consult with a competent attorney who knows the laws for your state. You will need to be of legal age in your state to complete these documents. Once you've done all this work, be sure to let the appropriate people know where to find the documents if required.

Do you know the old saying that, "Nothing in life is certain except death and taxes?" Well, we covered death, so let's move on to taxes.

Uncle Sam Is Not Your Friend

"The art of taxation consists in so plucking the goose as to obtain the largest
amount of feathers with the least possible amount of hissing."
— JEAN-BAPTISTE COLBERT

For most people, a discussion on taxes is about as exciting as surfing the web on a dial-up modem. Unless you're a math geek, it's hard to get the adrenaline flowing while pondering tax credits and deductions. Therefore, I recommend that you have two essential tools by your side before wading through this chapter:

1. Your salty snack of choice; and
2. Your favorite beverage.

I am a firm believer in paying every penny owed in taxes. At the same time, if you don't understand how the tax code works, you might make financial decisions that result in you paying more than necessary.

In addition, we will see later that Uncle Sam offers numerous tax-favored goodies that you might never realize were available unless you make the effort to learn about them. These items include various retirement programs, funding a college education, and tax-advantaged bonds, among others.

Were you shocked by how much was taken out of your first real paycheck? Me too. Of all your extended family members, it's your good ol' Uncle Sam who is most likely to have the greatest direct impact on your financial life. In fiscal year 2010, the United States government will spend $3.8 trillion dollars (yes, trillion) on our behalf. The money to fund the operation of the government comes out of your pocket and mine in the form of taxes.

Uncle Sam means well, but does tend to be somewhat fickle. Sometimes, he dreams up wonderful programs to encourage you to save, invest, go to college, buy electric cars, and so on. Other times, he realizes he needs a lot more money so he decides to raise taxes or eliminate (or change eligibility) for programs that are quite helpful to you.

The trick is to become aware of the myriad ways that Uncle Sam is both your best financial friend and a most annoying uncle, all at the same time.

To make this subject a bit more digestible, I have divided the Uncle Sam topics into two chapters. The bad news will come first. This chapter will focus on the basics of United States federal taxes. The chapter that follows will provide an overview of some of the goodies that can reduce your tax burden.

These include retirement plans, income tax deductions and credits, tax-advantaged bonds, and education savings plans.

Be aware Uncle Sam is both a referee and player in this game. He can modify the rules at any time. So, please understand that the details in these two chapters may have changed by the time you are reading this. The government adjusts annually for inflation, so the exact numbers I mention will likely be somewhat different depending upon the tax year in question. Congress may also decide to cancel, modify, or add new programs at any time. Further, you may one day find that suddenly your income is too high for some of the goodies the government offers.

Two of the key principles mentioned earlier were: (1) pay attention and (2) get ongoing financial education. These guidelines are particularly relevant for any government-related topic. My purpose in the next two chapters is to expose you to the basic concepts of taxes and the government programs that may affect you financially. However, I will not be covering everything, nor will I be going into detail. A great many books are devoted exclusively to the subject of taxes and this book is not one of them!

Do treat these two chapters as food for thought to help you understand the basic concepts behind the federal tax code and learn about some of the financial gifts available from Uncle Sam. Consider these reference chapters that you will want to go back to when needed. Consult with your accountant or favorite tax preparation software, as appropriate. With those caveats in mind, let's start with the topic that covers how Uncle Sam negatively affects your financial well-being. That topic, of course, is ... taxes.

The Short Story on Taxes

- The United States has a **progressive income tax** code. That means the government takes proportionally more in taxes as your income rises.
- **Regressive taxes**, like a tax on gasoline, are higher as a percentage of income for a poor person than a rich one.
- **Ordinary income** is income from sources like your wages at work and bank interest.
- **Capital gains** taxes apply for profitable sales of stocks, mutual funds, and the like.
- Uncle Sam taxes **ordinary income** at different rates than **capital gains** and **qualified stock dividends**.
- An **income tax deduction** is an eligible expense you may subtract from your gross income to reduce the income subject to tax.
- A **tax credit** is even better than a deduction because it is a direct reduction of your tax liability.
- Your **effective tax rate** is the amount of tax paid expressed as a percentage of your gross income.
- Your **marginal tax rate** is the tax rate that you're paying on the last dollar of taxable income.
- **Social Security** is the government's old age pension plan for your retirement; 6.2% of your wages (up to $106,800) is withheld from your paycheck to support this program.
- **Medicare** is the medical care plan for the elderly; 1.45% of your wage income is withheld to fund it.
- If you are **self-employed**, you must pay an additional 7.65% tax for the employer portion of Social Security and Medicare.
- Most states apply a **state income tax** on your earnings, capital gains, and dividends.
- The **Alternative Minimum Tax (AMT)** is a nasty little surprise that may await you as your income grows.

Read on for all the gruesome details!

The United States has a progressive income tax code. This means that an individual's tax rate increases as income rises. The intention is that rich people pay proportionally more than poor people.

You may also hear the term regressive tax, which indicates that the poor are affected more than the rich with a particular tax levy. For example, a gasoline tax can be considered regressive because it is proportionally higher as a percent of income for a poor person than a rich one.

Both progressive and regressive taxes are levied throughout your lifetime. Here's a rundown on the major taxes you will encounter.

Federal Income Tax

Income tax is the biggie. Every year by mid-April, you must file a tax return with the Internal Revenue Service (IRS) to report your income and to pay the appropriate tax due. If Uncle Sam was efficient, he would simply say, "Add up your income and send me X%—thank you very much, we really appreciate your support!"

Well, as you probably know, our taxation system is not that simple. Uncle Sam does not even tax all income at the same rate.

Ordinary income is income from sources like your wages from work and bank interest. The table that follows summarizes the income tax rates for ordinary income that are in effect for 2010. You might think you could simply go to this table, plug in your total income and you'd know your tax liability. Nope. There are a variety of adjustments to income, deductions, exemptions, and other things that keep your accountant very excited and well paid. We will discuss these later.

Ordinary Income Tax Rates and Amounts - 2010

Tax Rate	If Single and Taxable Income Is:	If Married Filing Jointly and Taxable Income Is:
10%	Not over $8,375	Not over $16,750
15%	On income between $8,375 and $34,000; plus $837.50	On income between $16,750 and $68,000; plus $1,675
25%	On income between $34,000 and $82,400; plus $4,681.25	On income between $68,000 and $137,300; plus $9,362.50
28%	On income between $82,400 and $171,850; plus $16,781.25	On income between $137,300 and $209,250; plus $26,687.50
33%	On income between $171,850 and $373,650; plus $41,827.25	On income between $209,250 and $373,650; plus $46,833.50
35%	On income over $373,650; plus $108,421.25	On income over $373,650; plus $101,085.50

To complicate things further, let's look at another category of income. **Capital gains** taxes apply for profitable sales of stocks, mutual funds, and the like. In 2010, the maximum tax on a long-term capital gain (for example, on a stock held more than a year) is only 15%. It can be as low as 0% depending on your income.

Similarly, qualified stock **dividends** are subject to the same rate as capital gains. (Corporations sometimes return a portion of their profits directly to shareholders. This payment is called a dividend and is typically paid in cash.) Compare those rates with the ordinary income tax rate table above and decide which rate you'd rather be paying! I don't know about you, but personally I'd rather be rich and living off my long-term capital gains and stock dividends rather than working for someone else all day long.

Believe it or not, the tax rates described above are relatively low compared to rates that were in place for the second half of the 20th century. For example, in 1980, the top income tax rate was 70%. In 1960 it was 91%!

The relatively low tax rates now in effect may not continue for long. Some of the tax rates for ordinary income, long-term capital gains, and dividends are scheduled to increase in 2011 unless Congress changes the law. Maybe they will. Maybe they won't. Pay attention, because any changes will have an impact on your wallet ... and your life.

Uncle Sam complicates things further by granting a variety of income tax deductions, credits, and exemptions that help you reduce your tax liability. We'll get into this in detail later. For now, here are some definitions that will be helpful:

- **Income tax deduction**: An eligible expense you can subtract from your gross income to reduce the income upon which tax liability is calculated. Examples include home mortgage interest and property taxes on your personal residence.
- A **tax credit** is even better than a deduction because it is a direct offset (reduction) of your tax liability. For example, if your tax due is $3,000 before the credit and you have a credit worth $1,000, then you would owe $2,000 instead.

With all these deductions, adjustments, and credits it gets a bit confusing to figure out what percentage of your gross income you are actually paying in federal income tax. Here are a couple of handy terms to help you do that:

- **Effective tax rate**: This is the amount of tax paid expressed as a percentage of your gross income. For example, if your income tax is $7,000 and your gross income is $50,000, then your effective tax rate is $7,000/$50,000 x 100 = 14%. This number can be helpful when preparing your budget for the next year if you expect your income will be approximately the same as the current year.
- **Marginal tax rate**: This is the tax rate that applies to the last "taxable dollar of income." For example, let's assume you're a single person with $50,000 per year of taxable income after you have subtracted your tax deductions, adjustments, and exemptions. If you look at the earlier table showing the 2010 tax rates, this would mean your marginal tax rate is 25%. Why would you care about this number? Well, if you get a raise at work, wouldn't it be helpful to know how much will go to Uncle Sam? In this example, if you were to get an annual raise of $1,000, you would pay 25% of that ($250) in federal income tax. It is also handy to know your marginal tax rate because it can help you figure out the value of a particular tax deduction. Notice, for example, that a deduction of $1,000 at a marginal rate of 25% is worth $250 in federal tax savings. It is only worth $150 if your marginal rate is 15%.

Social Security and Medicare Levies

Social Security is the government's old age pension plan for your retirement. Medicare is the medical care plan for the elderly. Also called "FICA" (Federal Insurance Contributions Act), funds are withheld from your paycheck for both of these. The amount is 7.65% (6.2% for Social Security plus 1.45% for Medicare).

Social Security is another example of a regressive tax. As a percentage of income, someone earning $30,000 per year actually pays more to Social Security than does someone earning $1,000,000 (or more). In 2010, Social Security withholding applies to the first $106,800 in wages (not to capital gains or dividends). Medicare is not subject to a wage limit.

Your employer must pay a matching amount. So, the total Social Security tax is 12.4% of wages and Medicare is 2.9%.

Self-Employment Tax

Want to be self-employed and stop working for "The Man?" Great! Just don't forget that you'll be subject to "Self-Employment Tax," which adds an additional 7.65% on top of the other stuff we've mentioned. When self-employed, you are both employee and employer, so you "get" to pay the matching amount that your employer would normally pay for Social Security and Medicare.

Alternative Minimum Tax (AMT)

Here's another big income tax item that may make you reach for the aspirin bottle: the dreaded AMT or "Alternative Minimum Tax." Odds are that this will not affect you in your early working years. However, you will need to watch out for it as your salary grows.

The AMT was originally aimed at very rich people who took advantage of so many deductions that they ended owing little or no tax. Ridiculously complicated, it is essentially a "parallel tax code" with its own set of deductions, exemptions, and tax rates.

Since the AMT does not adjust for inflation like the regular tax code, it is beginning to hit middle class wage earners, not just the rich. (Are you still with me or has your mind wandered off to a great fantasy about your latest love interest?)

With luck, Congress will finally fix this thing permanently. Sadly, I'm not putting my money on it. So, at some point in the future, your accountant or tax prep software may say, "You owe AMT this year!" You heard it here first.

State Income Taxes

In the discussion above, I have not made any mention of state income taxes because these levies vary from state to state. In fact, seven states have no state income tax: Alaska, Florida, Nevada, South Dakota, Texas, Washington and Wyoming. Two others, New Hampshire and Tennessee, tax only dividend and interest income. The remaining states do have some tax on income. In California where I live, the top rate is 10.55%. Ouch! Be sure to look up this information for your state and factor it into your calculations.

Yippee, I Got a Raise!

Now that we've covered marginal tax rates and have taken a look at the differences in tax rates for ordinary income and capital gains, let's see how this might play out in real life. Using our earlier example of a single person with $50,000 taxable income in 2010, let's compare three scenarios that highlight the potential variation in tax consequences when each earns an additional $1,000.

Our first person earns all his income from his work as a self-employed writer. The second is a graphic designer who earns all her income from wages as an employee. The third is living entirely off income produced by his trust fund's long-term capital gains and qualified dividend income. We'll assume that each person gets an increase of exactly $1,000 from the same sources. What will be the incremental tax liability of each?

Tax Liability From an Additional $1,000 in Tax Year 2010 Earnings, Assuming $50,000 Taxable Income

A Single Person	Self-Employed Wage Income Only	Wages From Employer Only	Income Entirely From Long-Term Capital Gains and Qualified Dividends
Federal income tax (25%)	$250	$250	$0
FICA (7.65%)	$0	$76.50	$0
Self-employment tax[5] (15.3%)	$153	$0	$0
Tax on qualified dividends and/or long-term capital gains (15%)	$0	$0	$150
Taxes due on the incremental $1,000	$403	$326.50	$150
Total percentage taken by taxes on the extra $1,000	40%	33%	15%

So, which column would you rather be in? Our lucky trust fund person got a raise of $1,000 and only had an additional $150 in federal tax liability, whereas the self-employed and salaried wage earner paid $403 and $326.50, respectively.

[5] Please note that half the self-employment tax is deductible so the total percentage taken by taxes is actually slightly less than the number above.

As of this writing, the capital gain and dividend tax rates are slated to increase in 2011, so the example may or may not be accurate beginning in 2011. Regardless, it is essential that you pay attention to income and capital gains tax rates because, as you can see, the impact on your wallet is pretty significant.

Adding It All Up

Let's think back on the information from the previous few pages.

Clearly, you will be handing over a lot of your money to Uncle Sam and your state tax authorities, so it's important to understand how this works. If you are currently employed, I would encourage you to look at your paycheck and tax returns and calculate how much you are paying for each of the tax items discussed in this chapter. Determine the total amount paid and the percentage of gross income for each item. Figure out your marginal and effective income tax rates for federal income taxes and, if applicable, your state income taxes.

Yes, taxes amount to a lot of money and are possibly one of your biggest expenses. Understanding how the tax system works will help you plan for and manage your tax liabilities. It will also help you make better financial decisions. For example, if you know your marginal tax bracket and are thinking of buying a house, you can accurately determine the tax savings that may result from the home's mortgage interest and property tax deduction.

Even better, there are a great number of provisions in the tax code that will help you financially, so developing detailed knowledge of the "good stuff" will be to your advantage. Let's talk about that next.

Uncle Sam Is Your Friend After All

"The art is not in making money, but in keeping it."
— PROVERB

Now that I've made your head hurt, it's time to move on to something more uplifting. You probably demolished the entire bag of your salty snacks while you read the last chapter. Depending on the contents of the beverage you consumed, you may or may not be in the mood to hear any more about Uncle Sam right now. (If that's the case, you have my permission to resume reading later.)

It turns out that Uncle Sam is not such an ogre after all. He is kind and benevolent in many ways. The government has put a bunch of goodies in the tax code that will make you smile. Let's take a tour through some of the common ones that may affect you.

The same admonitions apply as before. These may or may not exist beyond 2010 and I am only going to cover some of the more common items. It's possible that you may not be eligible for some of things we'll discuss here. Further, you may be able to take advantage of other tax-favored goodies that I don't mention. Consult with your accountant or favorite tax prep software to determine what is relevant for you.

The Short Story on Goodies From Uncle Sam

- You are a member of the "you're on your own" generation when it comes to retirement planning. The pension plans your parents depended on are disappearing.
- A **401(k)** is an employer-sponsored **defined contribution** plan that allows you to save for retirement and also save on the current year's taxes.
- Many employers will match your 401(k) contributions to some degree.
- You may be eligible to contribute to a traditional **Individual Retirement Account (IRA)**. Depending on your situation, you may save on the current year's income taxes by doing so. Your earnings inside the IRA will grow tax-deferred.
- A **Roth IRA** is funded with after-tax contributions. If you meet the criteria, your withdrawals can be tax-free!
- **Roth 401(k)** plans are employer-sponsored and are a hybrid of the 401(k) and the Roth IRA.
- An **income tax deduction** is an eligible expense you can subtract from your gross income to reduce the income upon which tax liability is calculated.
- A **tax credit** is even better than a deduction because it is a direct offset (reduction) of your tax liability.
- Many **tax-advantaged savings plans** are available to help you fund your education. These include: 529 plans, Coverdell Education Savings Accounts (ESA), and others.
- Qualified **municipal bonds** issued by local or state governments are exempt from federal, state, and local income taxes.
- **U.S. Treasury notes, bonds, and bills** are exempt from state and local income taxes.
- **U.S. Savings Bonds** are exempt from state and local income taxes. Federal taxes are deferred until the bonds are redeemed. They may also be tax-exempt if used to fund certain higher-education expenses.

Retirement Plans

During my parents' working years, people often worked for the same employer for life. The employer frequently offered a pension to cover the employee's financial needs during retirement. Over the last 30 years or so, these **defined benefit** pensions (a specific benefit amount paid in future years) have gradually been disappearing. Most employers no longer offer them. Increasingly, people are left to fend for themselves in retirement planning.

Social Security will hopefully provide some income when you're retired. You should be aware that it is not designed to cover all of one's financial needs. Further, it is woefully underfunded at the moment. It would be folly on your part to count on the full benefits that are currently available. It's probably very hard to think about retirement while in your 20s. I assure you that you'll be glad you took action on this early when you're in your 60s and beyond.

There are a number of tax-favored retirement plans out there. It is to your benefit to understand them and begin contributing NOW to any of the programs where you are eligible. Remember the time value of money principle that we discussed earlier in the book? This concept is highly relevant when you're thinking about funding retirement.

> *At age 21, if you put away $200 per month for 50 years and earn 8% in the stock market, you'll have $1,586,345 at age 71. If you contribute $500 per month, you'd be looking at nearly $4 million. By waiting until age 31, your balance will drop by 56%.*

Sorry to be annoying about this, but PLEASE don't let this opportunity pass you by! This is one of the few areas where the young have a huge advantage over those who are even slightly older. Many employers will match your contributions to their tax-favored retirement plans. Always contribute enough to get the company match! This is free money! Lastly, Uncle Sam has provided several benefits via the tax code to encourage you to save in this way. Here's an overview of the major tax-favored retirement plans:

Traditional 401(k) plan: A 401(k) is an employer-sponsored plan which allows you, the employee, to defer some of your compensation and with it, defer the current taxes that would have been otherwise due. Investment earnings generated inside the 401(k) are also tax deferred until the money is withdrawn.

Obviously, the person who thought up the name did not work for an ad agency. It comes from the part of the Internal Revenue Code that provides the legal basis for these plans ("Section 401, paragraph k").

A 401(k) is a **defined contribution** plan where the employer's contribution is specified, but the amount of the eventual payout is not. (Contrast this with the defined benefit retirement pension described earlier.) The future payout will depend upon on: (1) the total contributions from you and your employer; (2) the gains that accrue from the investments you select; and (3) the age at which you begin withdrawing money.

The tax deferral feature of a 401(k) is a great benefit. For example, let's say you have $6,000 ($500 per month) that you could either take as wage income this year or defer it through a 401(k) plan. We'll assume that the marginal tax bracket for the entire $6,000 contribution is 25%. (Aha! The first real-world application of the marginal tax rate we discussed last chapter!) Let's look at the impact that each alternative might have on your annual cash flow[6]:

Annual Change in Cash Flow

	With 401(k) Contribution	Without 401(k) Contribution
Federal Income Tax Due Now on the $6,000	$0	$1,500
Amount Available To Invest	$6,000	$4,500 ($6,000 less $1,500 tax paid)

Uncle Sam is loaning you the money that he otherwise would have collected in taxes this year so that you may invest it for your retirement. The result is that only $4,500 of the annual contribution comes from you in this example. The remaining $1,500 is loaned from Uncle Sam. So, when considering how much you can afford to contribute, you want to think about the after-tax amount ($375 per month or $4,500 annually in this case), not the before-tax amount ($500 per month or $6,000 annually).

Note that "tax deferral" does not mean you escape taxes on the money forever. When you withdraw the money, you are subject to ordinary income taxes at the rate that's in effect at the time of withdrawal. Generally speaking, you cannot withdraw the money before age 59½ without paying a 10% penalty (plus the normal taxes due). There are certain exceptions to this rule, but it's best you think of this money as unavailable until retirement.

In 2010, you can contribute up to $16,500 to your 401(k); more if you are

[6] *If your state has an income tax, you may receive an additional benefit from the state income tax deferral.*

over age 50. If your employer matches some of the dollars that you elect to defer into your 401(k) account, TAKE THE MONEY! This is a gift that you will not want to walk away from. I'll say it again: this is FREE MONEY! At a minimum, contribute the amount required to get the full match from your employer. Of course, use common sense here. If you have to run up a balance on your credit card to do this, then postpone your 401(k) contributions until you have your spending under control. (Refer to Chapter 6 "*Spending*" for ideas on modifying your spending habits to make money available for retirement savings.)

By the way, if you work for a non-profit entity, your employer may offer a "403(b)" plan, which shares many similarities with the 401(k) plans offered in the corporate world. Read your plan's literature for more information.

"Traditional" Individual Retirement Account (IRA): This refers to the original IRA plan, which allows you to set aside up to $5,000 per year ($6,000 if you're over age 50). You must have income from wages (e.g., not stock sales, dividends, and the like) to contribute in a given tax year. If you are married and your spouse does not work, he or she is generally eligible to contribute to an IRA as well. This means that you and your spouse together may be eligible to contribute up to $10,000/year ($12,000 if you are both over age 50). You may be eligible to deduct some or all of your contributions on your tax return, depending on your income level and whether you are covered by a qualified retirement plan at your employer. (Tax deductions will be covered in more detail later in this chapter.)

Any earnings in an IRA account are tax deferred until you begin withdrawals, at which time you pay ordinary income tax on the distributions. Generally speaking, if you withdraw the money before age 59½ you will be subject to a 10% penalty in addition to ordinary income taxes. Distributions must begin by the time you reach age 70½. Assuming you are eligible for a tax deduction, the same tax deferral benefits described in the 401(k) paragraphs also apply here.

"Non-deductible" IRA: This is similar to a traditional IRA. The difference is you are not allowed to deduct contributions on your current year income tax return. (The term is a bit misleading, because it is possible to have "partially deductible" contributions depending on your income level.) A deduction is typically disallowed because your income is too high and/or you have a qualified retirement plan available to you at work. So, your contribution comes from after-tax money. ("After-tax" refers to income on which you have already paid taxes.)

If you cannot deduct your contributions, it may still make sense to fund a non-deductible IRA. The reason is that earnings generated by the account receive the same beneficial tax deferral as a deductible IRA. When you begin withdrawals from the account, your original contribution comes out tax-free. Any gains from the account are subject to ordinary income tax. Most other aspects of non-deductible IRAs are the same as the traditional IRA plans.

Roth IRA: This is an after-tax retirement savings vehicle that is named after the late Senator William Roth, who was one of the chief sponsors of the legislation that established them. You will have already paid taxes on the income used to fund the account. However, the huge benefit of Roth IRAs is that any gains the account generates are completely tax-free as long as you meet certain conditions.

Unlike a traditional IRA, you are not forced to begin distributions at a certain date. You can leave the money there your entire life if you choose or pass it on to your heirs. The amount you can contribute to a Roth IRA is similar to the limits for a traditional IRA. However, a big drawback is that eligibility to contribute to a Roth IRA phases out if your income rises above certain limits.

Roth IRAs may be particularly advantageous if you expect that your tax rate in retirement will be greater than the tax rate in effect during the years you made the contributions. If you are in one of the lower tax brackets at the beginning of your working years it might be to your benefit to emphasize Roth IRAs early on by paying taxes on the contributions upfront and then escaping taxes at the end after amassing a huge pile of cash in the account over your working lifetime. (This is another example of why it is handy to know your marginal tax rate.)

You'll have to do the future tax bracket guesswork on your own, depending on what your crystal ball tells you. Finally, be aware that tax law allows for a process to "convert" a traditional IRA to a Roth IRA, which may be worth considering at some point. That's something you'd want to discuss with a tax professional. The analysis is too complicated to go into detail here. Just be aware that the choice exists.

Roth 401(k): This one actually comes from Section 402A of the Internal Revenue code (go figure). These are employer-sponsored plans named after the same Senator William Roth of Roth IRA fame. Roth 401(k) plans are an interesting hybrid of the Roth IRA and the regular 401(k). As with a Roth IRA, the contributions you make are on an after-tax basis. Withdrawals are generally tax free at retirement, subject to certain conditions.

Roth 401(k) plans do not subject the employee to the same income limitations as a Roth IRA. They also allow much higher contributions (up to $16,500 in 2010; $22,000 if you are over age 50) than the Roth IRA.

If your employer offers a Roth 401(k) in addition to the traditional 401(k), it is possible to contribute to both. However, your combined contributions may not exceed these limits. As with the Roth IRA, the Roth 401(k) may be particularly attractive if you think your tax rate in retirement will be higher than it is when you are making the contributions.

SIMPLE IRA and SEP-IRA plans: These are both employer-sponsored plans for smaller businesses. They offer simplified administration for the employer when compared with some other retirement plans. The SIMPLE acronym stands for "Savings Incentive Match Plan for Employees." SEP stands for "Simplified Employee Pension."

If you are employed at a company that offers one of these, review the plan literature for details. Also, IRS Publication 560 (**www.irs.gov**) covers these plans in more detail. Though they differ somewhat in the specifics when compared with 401(k) and other employer-sponsored retirement plans, both SIMPLE and SEP plans are intended to help provide retirement benefits for the employee and for the self-employed.

That completes our flyby of some of the tax-advantaged retirement plans that might be available to you. Remember that this was just a basic introduction. As with most government creations, there are many exceptions, restrictions, eligibility requirements, and various other rules that you'll need to be aware of before plunging forth with contributions. For more information, consult the following sources:

- For employer-sponsored plans such as a 401(k), refer to the plan literature that the company provides to you.
- The IRS provides a couple of publications that you should look over (available at **www.irs.gov**):
  ◦ IRS Publication 560, *"Retirement Plans for Small Business"* covers SEP, SIMPLE, and other qualified plans typically sponsored by smaller employers.
  ◦ IRS Publication 590, *"Individual Retirement Arrangements"* explains traditional IRAs, Roth IRAs, and SIMPLE IRAs.
  ◦ Most brokerage firms and mutual fund companies have a wealth of literature that explains the details in plain English. You'll need to work with one of them anyway as they'll be the "custodian" of your IRA once you decide to open an account. The investing section of this book has more information on working with brokerages and fund companies.
- Finally, I have listed a variety of additional resources on my website that you might also want to examine.

Later in the book (the "*Investing*" section) we'll talk about options for where you might invest the money that you have directed to these plans.

> *The most important part to remember about this section*
> *on retirement plans is this: if you are eligible for a retirement plan,*
> *be sure to contribute. This is especially true of any plan*
> *with an employer match. Then, leave the money alone*
> *until you are ready for retirement.*

Income Tax Deductions

Let's move to a variety of **tax deductions** and adjustments to income that might benefit you during income tax filing season. A deduction or adjustment is an amount of money you can subtract from your income to reduce the income subject to tax. The amount of tax saved is dependent on your marginal tax rate. (There it is again!) The higher your tax bracket, the better the tax savings.

Here is a sampling of common income tax deductions or adjustments to income that you might find advantageous if you qualify to take them:

- Personal exemptions for yourself, spouse, and dependents. Each exemption reduces your income by $3,650 in 2010. (These exemptions phase out if your income is too high.)
- Contributions to an Individual Retirement Account (IRA)
- Certain educator expenses if you are a teacher
- Health Savings Account (HSA) contributions
- Moving expenses
- Student loan interest
- Tuition and fees
- Self-employed health insurance

Most of these items are called above-the-line deductions because they are literally right above the line on the tax form for your adjusted gross income. These are generally more valuable than below-the-line deductions because they directly reduce the amount of income subject to tax. Below-the-line deductions are a bit trickier and here's an oversimplified explanation of why.

The IRS allows a **standard deduction** to further reduce your taxable income. In 2010, if you are single, the standard deduction is $5,700. If you are married filing jointly, the standard deduction is $11,400. That's right, just by having a pulse, the IRS lets you subtract either $5,700 (single) or $11,400 (married filing jointly) from your adjusted gross income, and so that amount will not be taxed. How nice!

But wait, there's more! Instead of taking a standard deduction, you may be eligible to use **itemized deductions** instead. Many of these below-the-line deductions are reported on Form 1040 Schedule A, *"Itemized Deductions."* Here is a partial list of deductions that can be itemized:

- Home mortgage interest
- Property tax on your residence
- State and local income taxes
- New motor vehicle taxes
- Gifts to charity
- Casualty and theft losses
- Tax preparation fees
- Medical and dental expenses that exceed 7.5% of your income

To determine whether to use the itemized deductions, you simply tally up all the eligible items you have on Schedule A. If the itemized deductions exceed the standard deduction, you use the itemized deductions. Otherwise, you take the standard deduction.

Have you figured out why below-the-line deductions are less valuable than above-the-line deductions? Here's the answer. Until your itemized deductions (which are below the line) exceed your standard deduction, they are not worth anything. The itemized deductions begin to have value once their total amount starts to exceed the standard deduction. If they don't exceed it, then they are worthless to you.

Jack and Jill Want to Buy a House

Here is an example of how to use your knowledge of tax deductions. Let's say Jack and Jill want to buy a house. They have heard they can deduct their property tax and mortgage interest expense, so they are hoping that the tax savings from this deduction will help them afford the house. They will pay $10,000 in property tax and mortgage interest. They have $1,000 in other deductible expenses for a total of $11,000 in itemized deductions. Jack and Jill are married, so their standard deduction is $11,400. Does the deduction for mortgage interest and property tax help them? The answer is "no" because the total amount of their itemized deductions ($11,000) does not exceed the standard deduction ($11,400).

Let's modify the example slightly. Let's say that the itemized deductions that Jack and Jill have with the new house expenses total $12,000 instead of $11,000. In this case, the advantage from the itemized deductions is only $600 ($12,000 - $11,400). If the entire $600 falls into a marginal tax rate of 25%, then the federal tax savings on this deduction is $150 ($600 x .25). The tax deduction they thought would help them doesn't really do much in this case, does it? It's a good thing they ran the numbers before buying the house or they might have been in for a rude surprise if they were expecting big tax savings.

Biff and Buffy Buy a House

Let's do one final example to see how itemizing can be really helpful. Our friends Biff and Buffy, a married couple, want to buy a house. They have a good income and pay a lot of income tax to the state of California. Luckily for them, state income tax is deductible on their federal tax return. The sum of all their eligible deductions prior to the house purchase is currently $12,000. This number is above the standard deduction, so they are itemizing.

Biff and Buffy decide to buy a beachfront hovel in Newport Beach for $800,000. (This price is probably a bit low for a hovel in Newport Beach, but never mind.) Let's say that this year's deductible property tax and mortgage interest expense is $40,000. Assume the entire amount falls in the 28% marginal tax bracket.

Since they have crossed the threshold to fully utilize the itemized deductions, the federal tax savings resulting from house-related deductions is $11,200 ($40,000 x .28). They would also get an additional benefit of over $3,500 savings in state income taxes. Not bad!

Of course, this assumes that the AMT does not now ensnare them (see previous chapter). If I started talking about that, I'm sure you'd pour another glass of your favorite beverage or tune this out completely. So I'll spare you that dissertation.

Tax Credits

A tax deduction reduces the amount of income subject to tax. A **tax credit**, on the other hand, is a direct offset (reduction) of your tax liability. For example, if your tax due is $3,000 before the credit and you have a credit worth $1,000, then you would owe $2,000 instead. If you're eligible, tax credits can save you lots of money. Here's a partial list:
- Child and dependent care expenses: provides you a credit toward some of the day care expenses you may have while working or looking for work.
- Child tax credit: this is worth up to $1,000 per child!
- Energy saving home improvements credit.
- Various higher education credits, like the Hope credit and Lifetime

Learning credit.

- To encourage the purchase of more electric cars, a tax credit of up to $7,500 is available for purchase of those vehicles.

I will again caution you that the tax deductions and credits described above come with many strings attached: income limitations, restrictions on when/how they can be taken, and so on. I highlight them here so you have an idea of what might be available. You should do more research or consult with a tax advisor to determine what might be relevant for you.

Education Savings Plans

529 accounts: Remember how 401(k) plans were named after that section of the Internal Revenue Code? Yes, you guessed it. We have an education savings plan named after its very own section of that same code.

Like a Roth IRA, 529 plan contributions are funded with after-tax money. Any earnings that might accrue in the account are tax free if used for college tuition or other qualified education expenses. Earnings that are used for other reasons are subject to ordinary income tax and a 10% penalty. Anyone can establish and contribute to a 529 account, regardless of age or income. Some states provide an income tax deduction on contributions, so check out the rules in your location. Section 529 savings plans are sponsored by states, which generally delegate management and investment choices to a financial services company. For more information, visit **www.savingforcollege.com** for detailed explanations of how 529 plans work and ratings for each state's plan.

Education Savings Accounts (ESA): Also known as Coverdell ESA, this plan allows eligible people to contribute up to $2,000 a year through 2010 to an account to encourage saving for college expenses. Contributions are not tax deductible. Any gains grow tax deferred and distributions are tax exempt for qualified education expenses. Note that your income must be below statutory limits to contribute. In 2011, the amount you may contribute is scheduled to drop to $500 annually and certain benefits will be curtailed unless Congress acts to extend the current amounts and benefits. Stay tuned.

U.S. Savings Bonds: These are not an education savings plan, per se. I mention them here because the interest earned on Series EE and Series I Savings Bonds can be exempt from federal income tax under certain circumstances if the proceeds are used to pay for your education or your child's education. More information is below and at **www.savingsbonds.gov**.

The IRS has a helpful document that explains these and other education related programs, tax credits, and deductions. Go to **www.irs.gov** and search for Publication 970, "*Tax Benefits for Education*."

Other Tax-Advantaged Items

Gain on sale of residence: If you own your home and have lived in it as your principal residence for two of the last five years, you may be able to avoid capital gains taxes on the property (up to a limit) if you have a profit upon sale. You can exclude up to $250,000 in profits as an individual or $500,000 as a married couple.

Municipal bonds: Qualified bonds issued by local or state governments are exempt from federal, state, and local income taxes.

U.S. Treasuries: Among the safest investments in the world (for now, anyway) are bonds, notes, and bills offered by the United States Treasury. Issued in maturities ranging from a few days to 30 years, they merit a mention in this section because the interest earned is exempt from state and local income taxes if those are levied where you live. Therefore, the after-tax yield on Treasuries is likely a bit higher than, say, a bank-issued CD with the same interest rate that is subject to those taxes.

We'll discuss bonds in more detail in the section on investing. For now, just be aware that the exemption from state and local income tax is one of Uncle Sam's gifts to you if you choose to buy these securities. More information is available at **www.treasurydirect.gov**.

U.S. Savings Bonds (Series EE and Series I): Backed by the full faith and credit of the federal government, savings bonds are a super-safe place to stash excess cash. The Treasury issues two different versions: the more traditional Series EE and an inflation-adjusted Series I. They share the following characteristics:

- Issued in denominations as low as $25, so you don't need a huge amount of money to buy them.
- They can be purchased through a variety of financial institutions or directly from the U.S. Treasury.
- A purchase limit of $5,000 per year per Social Security number. (You can buy $5,000 each of Series EE and Series I if you want.)
- Interest compounds semi-annually for 30 years. You must hold them a minimum of one year. If you redeem them during the first five years, there is a 3-month interest penalty.
- They are exempt from state and local income taxes, so your after-tax yield (percentage return) is somewhat higher if you live in a jurisdiction that has these levies.
- Federal taxes are deferred until you cash them, which means you can control when the tax liability is incurred.
- Under certain circumstances, the interest earned is tax exempt if the proceeds are used to pay educational expenses for you or your children.

There are important distinctions between the Series EE and Series I Bonds. Series EE Bonds purchased on or after May 1, 2005, earn a fixed rate of return for the life of the bond. The Treasury posts this information online so you will know the interest rate in advance. If interest rates are exceptionally low when purchased, these might not be a particularly good investment if you intend to hold them for a very long time.

The Series I is a different animal. The interest rate it pays has two components: (1) a fixed rate that is set for the life of the bond; and (2) an "inflation uplift" that pays an additional amount based on changes in the Consumer Price Index (CPI-U). This is a great advantage because it provides you with some protection against rising inflation.

The Treasury announces the fixed rate twice a year. I'm not sure what their magic formula is for determining this rate. (I envision some bureaucrat rubbing his tummy and chanting a mantra until he is enlightened with the number.) It has ranged from 0% to 3.6% over the past 10 years. For more information on both Series EE and Series I Bonds, visit **www.savingsbonds.gov**.

I must confess I have a warm place in my heart for the Series I Bonds that my wife and I purchased 10 years ago. At the time, the dot-com era was in full swing and any stock that had anything to do with an online presence was rocketing skyward. Very few people had any interest in dowdy Savings Bonds. I happened to read an article in a personal finance magazine that Uncle Sam was offering a 3.6% fixed rate plus the variable inflation add-on. The author had suggested that a 3.6% return above the rate of inflation was a pretty good deal. Serendipitously, my credit card issuer sent a brochure around the same time offering double airline miles on any purchase within the next 60 days.

Well, smelling a good deal, I bought the maximum amount allowed. (In the year 2000, it was $30,000 per Social Security number.) I timed it to buy the bonds on the first day of my monthly credit card cycle so that I would get several weeks of free interest while I awaited my credit card bill. The icing on the cake was we got enough frequent flyer miles to earn two free first-class tickets to Hawaii.

Ten years later, these "boring" bonds are now worth $109,008, an 82% gain. Had I invested that $60,000 in an S&P 500® stock market index fund during that same period, I would have actually lost money. Sadly, this jackpot cannot be replicated now for a variety of reasons:

- The Treasury stopped accepting credit cards for payment a few years ago. You must now have the money debited from your checking or savings account.
- The government reduced the amount you can buy from $30,000/year per Social Security number to only $5,000.
- The fixed rate is currently a paltry 0.20%. When you add in the bond's adjustment inflation component the yield is only 1.74%.

So, why do I share this story and why should you care?

- At any given time, there's always an unloved asset class that no one wants to buy. That's often the time to investigate.
- The old parable about the tortoise and the hare running a race has some value. Sometimes a boring investment can be one of the best.
- Remember the *"Pay Attention"* and *"Continuously Educate Yourself"* principles we talked about earlier? I'm constantly scanning several personal finance periodicals and books and nearly always pick up some nugget of useful information. Sometimes I'll file it away for future research; sometimes (like this one), it spurs me to action.
- Finally, I was just so darn pleased with this that I had to share it. Since I will share many boneheaded things I've done with my money, I wanted to give you at least one story to show that I did things right. Thank you for humoring me.

Phew! We made it! The entire topic of taxes and tax-advantaged savings programs is horrifically complicated and could be the subject of an entire book. That is why many people hand the entire mess to their accountant once a year. Tax preparation software is also extremely helpful if you like to do your own taxes. Even so, sometimes it's beneficial to know what's available before the software or your accountant can help you take advantage of these things.

Yes, nothing in life is certain other than death and taxes. However, having a basic understanding of the tax code, your marginal tax bracket, and the goodies available from Uncle Sam will help you potentially reduce your overall tax liability. This knowledge will also help you make better financial decisions. (Our house purchase example with Jack and Jill is a good illustration.) I hope this demonstrates that the time invested to understand all this is time well spent.

To those of you who hung with me throughout the last two chapters, congratulations! You've learned an important component of the game of personal finance. To those who drifted off to fantasyland, I understand. This stuff is not easy to digest on the first pass. I'd encourage you use these chapters as a resource in the future. In addition, don't hesitate to discuss your situation with a good Certified Public Accountant (CPA) or

Certified Financial Planner® (CFP) if you continue to find this topic overwhelming in its complexity.

Advice from a trained professional may well be worth the expense and may help save you money in the long run. If you choose this route, I'd strongly encourage you to continue educating yourself so that you know what questions to ask and will be better positioned to understand what your CPA or CFP® is talking about.

Spending and Saving

> *"Never spend your money before you have it."*
> – THOMAS JEFFERSON

CHAPTER 6

Spending Your Way to Financial Freedom

"Creditors have better memories than debtors."
– BENJAMIN FRANKLIN

The title of this chapter is indeed an oxymoron. After several years of spending more money than was necessary, I finally realized that spending choices make a big difference at the end of the game. This should have been obvious to me early on. I just started on autopilot—spending without thinking about how much things cost and how I might spend less or not at all.

All of us make choices to spend our money in different ways. You will find in the following pages, for example, that I am not a big fan of expensive cars or designer clothes. I spend about $300 per year on my wardrobe. However, I spend 25 times that on travel. While I might playfully tease you about spending buckets of money on cars and clothing, you could do the same for my travel habit.

It doesn't matter to me where you spend your money. What I do care about is that you consistently end each month with more money in your pocket than when you started. If I were your kindly Uncle Jim, I would tell you to go out and have fun. Spend your money on things that bring you happiness. However, if your kindly uncle noticed you were always running out of money and piling on the debt, you and I would have a very different conversation.

This section of the book surveys the typical places where people spend their money. Your largest expense is likely to be housing, especially if you decide to buy a place of your own. Expenses related to your car will probably be your second biggest outlay. Each of these is important enough to warrant a lengthy discussion. The next two chapters will do that.

This chapter will focus on the smaller stuff. You might not think the little purchases matter in the grand scheme of things. After you finish this chapter, I am hoping you think differently about that.

Consider the dozens of purchasing transactions you make every month. Some of these items are mandatory; others are discretionary. Each requires cash, even if put on credit or otherwise financed. Once that money is gone, it's gone forever.

Even small expenses that don't seem like much are pretty significant when you annualize the cost. For example, that daily $1.25 can of soda I used to buy from the vending machine at work ends up being about $300/year! That same amount invested annually over a 50-year working lifetime is nearly $200,000. So while you may be tempted to think of that soda (or coffee, candy bar, or beer) as a trivial expense, the reality is, it's not!

The Lowdown on Spending

I wrote several of Chapter 2's *"Key Principles"* with spending in mind. They are handy guideposts you can consult to help manage monthly cash flow. Specifically:

- **Principle #2** ("Avoid bad debt; use good debt sparingly"): Don't buy anything you can't afford to pay off in full by the time your credit card bill arrives. Period. If you can't do this, use a debit card or pay cash for all your transactions. The major exceptions are student loans and house purchases.
- **Principle #3** ("Distinguish between wants and needs"): Other than food, shelter, simple clothing, insurance, and basic transportation, the list of needs is really short. It's fine to satisfy some of your "wants" if you can afford them after basic necessities and savings are covered.
- **Principle #4** ("Never pay full retail price for anything"): Yes, I really mean this literally. There are always deals to be had. Be sure to find them. Why would you want to give away more of your hard-earned cash than required? A significant portion of this chapter is devoted to helping you with this. A tip: sales can be dangerous. Saving 50% on an article of clothing that wasn't in your budget to begin with isn't going to help you in the long run. (You saved, but you still spent.)
- **Principle #5** ("Pay attention"): Most of us lead busy, harried lives. That makes it easy to make impulse purchases, neglect the fine print, forget to evaluate alternatives, avoid due diligence when required, and take the first offer that comes along. Not routinely paying attention can be very costly.
- **Principle #6** ("Develop good financial habits"): There are several things in your financial life that need to become as routine as brushing your teeth. (We're still working with the seven-year-old on that one.) These things include budgeting, paying the credit card in full every month, saving at least 10% of income, and always looking for the best deals. If you do them often enough they will become automatic reflexes and your financial life will just keep getting better and better.

Exit the Month With More Money
Than You Had at the Beginning of the Month

At the end of the month, your goal is to have more money in your pocket than you did when you started. As the old saying goes, "It doesn't matter how much you make, it matters how much you keep."

While accumulating savings is an essential element of achieving financial freedom, you obviously want to enjoy life along the way. Don't deny yourself the things you really want. Otherwise, you could end up like the perpetual dieter who starves for weeks, then binges on bags of chips and pans of brownies after the diet is "over." Here's the process that has worked for me:

1. Send 10% of your gross pay to an automatic savings account so that you never even see it (thank you, direct deposit).
2. Fund the essentials next (rent, insurance, groceries, etc.)
3. Spend on the "nice to have" items with the money that's left (travel, entertainment, cable TV, etc.).
4. Before purchasing anything, relentlessly review the price options or comparison shop to pay the least amount possible. The Internet makes this really easy.
5. At month end, review bank and credit card statements to see what expenses could be eliminated or reduced.
6. Send half the leftover money to savings.

Your Goal

Always be thinking about how to spend less than full price on every single expense (or whether you can eliminate the expense entirely), no matter how insignificant it might seem!

My wife and I started this process over 10 years ago when we were living in San Francisco. In our first year, we identified hundreds of dollars a month in spending that was "leaking" out of our pockets. That's over $10,000 a year! Later in this chapter I will share some of the ideas that helped us generate this savings.

Even today, we continue these reviews at regular intervals and are still finding spending that is wasteful, sloppy, or can be eliminated. For example, during our annual medical insurance renewal period this year, we realized we could save $100 per month by removing our son from our "family" policy and covering him as an individual. When we first signed up for coverage three years ago, we noted that "family" coverage was for subscriber, spouse, and one

---

or more children. If we had been paying more attention, we would have noticed the family coverage was a great deal if we had two or more kids. Since we have only one, we were overpaying by not covering him separately. So now, the three of us still have exactly the same coverage but we are saving $1,200 per year.

Over the last three years, we wasted over $3,500 by not configuring the policies this way from the beginning. That was an expensive lesson on the consequences of not paying attention.

Over time, this process has become a great game for me. I actually love it! (Admittedly less so for my wife, who once said, "You know, sometimes you're so tight you squeak.") I spend freely on things I view as important, like my son's education and his extracurricular activities. Everything else gets carefully scrutinized. Don't get me wrong. I spend plenty of money on stuff that's not essential. For example, I say goodbye to lots of cash on travel-related expenses. However, I also know I'm quite good at getting exceptionally good deals. So my frugal genes happily mesh with my need to see the world.

It's the same with everything else I buy. I purchase all the things I need and most of the things I want and am delighted knowing I got the best possible price. At the end of the month, the excess cash goes to our investment accounts so it can be put to work for the future.

The rest of this chapter, therefore, is devoted to helping you identify opportunities for "spending your way to financial freedom." I've bundled these into several categories for your review. Take a look at each one and decide whether it might be relevant for you. If so, I'd suggest the following:

1. Estimate your monthly and yearly savings if you were to move forward with that particular savings idea. For example, "By bringing soda with me to work rather than buying it from the vending machine, my cost goes from $1.25 per can to $0.25. Therefore, I save $22.00 per month or $264 per year."

2. Add it to a spreadsheet that looks something like this:

Category	Expense Item	Monthly Savings	Annual Savings
Beverages	Bring soda to work ($.25/can) instead of buying from vending machine at $1.25.	$22.00	$264.00
	Switch from daily cappuccino to brewed coffee.	$33.00	$396.00
Etc...			

3. After you get through the entire list, total up the monthly and annual savings. My hunch is that, for many of you, the annual savings will easily exceed $1,000. Depending upon your current income and spending habits, it could be a lot more.

4. Decide which ones you intend to implement. You don't necessarily need to do all of them at once, but you won't make any progress unless you act. Check off the items you've completed and tally up your actual savings.

5. Repeat the process at regular intervals. I've been doing this for over 10 years now and am still finding savings opportunities.

6. Direct at least half of the newly found cash to savings then spend the rest on things you haven't had enough money for!

Every time my wife and I do this, we find it quite motivating. We think of it as "mining for gold" instead of "cutting expenses." Thousands of dollars a year stay in our pockets that otherwise would have been gone for good. Some of that cash has been redirected to more travel and fun. The rest has been redeployed to our investment accounts. The savings motivated us to continue the process on a regular basis. It's now just an automatic part of how we manage our spending. I hope you find this equally motivating, as it will make a huge difference to your financial life.

The savings ideas that follow are grouped by expense category for your convenience. They are intended to:

1. Help you free up more money for things you like to do;
2. Assist with your savings efforts;

3. Help you reduce spending to get out of debt.

I don't want to leave you with the impression that you should implement all these ideas right away. Rather, scan the list and choose the items that you'd like to try and ignore the others or come back to them later. Remember, I've been at this for many years now and am still "mining for gold." You should proceed at whatever pace works for you. Here we go:

Financial Services
(Banks, Insurance, Investment Companies, Etc.)

Banking: Use a bank or credit union that does not charge nuisance fees (monthly account fee, minimum balance fees, ATM fees, etc.). There is no reason to support institutions that do this. Similarly, make sure your bank offers free online bill pay for time efficiency and to save on stamps. Never use an ATM that charges a fee. See the "Getting Started" chapter for details. Manage your money so you never get charged for overdrafts and other mistakes.

Credit cards: Always pay your credit card bill in full and on time every month. Late fees and interest expense on credit cards are horrible-they will suck money out of your pocket faster than most dogs can clean food scraps off the kitchen floor. Find a card that does not charge an annual fee and which gives you cash back for purchases. That is free money! Bankrate.com™ has a service that helps you search for credit cards with these types of features.

Products with sales commissions: Your warning antennae should go up when someone is trying to sell you a product on commission. This includes some banking products, certain mutual funds, insurance products, full service stockbrokers, and the like. The advice may be worth it, but know what you are paying for it. There are many good, reputable people who sell products with this type of compensation scheme. All I'm saying is be cautious. Make sure the product being promoted is indeed the best one for you. If I'm not sure how someone is compensated, I don't hesitate to ask if it is relevant to helping me make a purchase decision. I also inquire about all the relevant fees that are attached. Educate yourself in advance so that you are a well-informed consumer.

Insurance deductibles: Consider increasing the deductibles on your various insurance policies if you are willing to assume a bit more financial risk. Increasing the deductible may significantly reduce the premium you have to pay. The downside, of course, is that you will have to pay more out of your own pocket if a covered event like an accident should occur. (How is your emergency fund looking?) Your insurance agent can review the pros and cons with you.

Health insurance: If your employer does not provide coverage, comparison shop with a good independent insurance agent or try **www.ehealthinsurance.com**. Be sure to read the fine print. Make sure the coverage is suitable for your needs. If you are healthy and willing to assume more financial risk, you might consider an HSA-eligible "High Deductible Health Plan" (HDHP) paired with a "Health Savings Account" (HSA). Remember that "high-deductible" means that you are responsible for paying out-of-pocket up to a fairly high threshold if you need to use the services of a medical provider. In return, these plans typically have lower premiums than more traditional policies. Not all high-deductible plans are compatible with the use of an HSA, so be careful.

An HSA allows you to put pre-tax money into a special account that can be used to pay for eligible medical, dental, and vision expenses. Pre-tax money means you can save on federal income tax if you put cash into the HSA. (For example, if you are single and contribute the 2010 maximum of $3,050 to your HSA, you will save $762.50 in federal taxes if you are in the 25% marginal tax bracket.) You may also be able to save on state income tax if your state allows it. Any interest on the account is tax free if you use the money for qualified medical expenses. If you use the money for ineligible expenses, you will have to pay ordinary income tax plus a 10% penalty if withdrawn before age 65. Any money not used in one year simply rolls over for use in future years. It's like an IRA for health care. See IRS Publication 969 (**www.irs.gov**) for details and all the rules. Discuss the pros and cons with both an independent insurance agent and your tax pro to decide if this might be right for you.

Housing

- When you first start out, sharing an apartment with a friend is a great way to reduce your housing outlay. Even better, rent a house with two or three others. The first four years of my working life I shared a house with friends. The places we lived were some of the best neighborhoods on the San Francisco peninsula and yet we each paid far less than the cost of an apartment. We also saved a bundle on utility bills since the cost was shared among all of us. I also learned to cook from people who knew what they were doing!
- Look for move-in specials.
- Negotiate the down payment, security deposit, and other fees.
- Live near work, if possible, to avoid wasting time and money on commuting. Even better, live close enough to walk or bike to work!

Utilities (Energy)

- In winter, set the heat at no higher than 68°. In summer, set the air conditioner at 78° or higher. I know it sounds painful, but don't use the air conditioner unless absolutely necessary—it is a huge energy consumer and you'll really notice it on your electric bill!
- Get a programmable electronic thermostat or be diligent about adjusting the thermostat when you leave home or go to bed. Adjust temperature settings for nighttime and during periods you're at work so you're not paying for heat or A/C 24 hours a day.
- Change the furnace filter at recommended intervals.
- Swap out the old-fashioned incandescent light bulbs and replace them with compact fluorescent bulbs or LED bulbs. These are far more efficient and last much longer. Though the upfront cost is higher, you'll save lots of money over the life of each bulb. (Depending on electric rates where you live, this could be up to $50 for every bulb!)
- Weather-strip around leaky windows and doors.
- Run the dishwasher only when it's full.
- Turn off things that aren't in use. This includes the little vampires like the DVR that is flashing 12:00am on the clock, various devices on perpetual standby, and the like.
- Get rid of the second refrigerator in the garage or the mini-fridge under your desk.
- Consider turning down the temperature on your hot water heater. Use the unit's vacation setting if you'll be away from home for several days.
- For more ideas, visit **www.energysavers.gov**, a website sponsored by the U.S. Department of Energy.

Telecommunications (Phone, Internet, Cable TV)

- Get a quote for buying all as a bundle from the same company.
- Play one company off another. The competition is ruthless. Providers are often willing to match or beat a competitor's price. For example, I am currently paying 30% off the list price of my DSL service because I negotiated this way.
- Take a careful look at your landline (if you have one) and wireless service plans. Do you really need everything that you are paying for? Are you taking advantage of discounts that may be available for the numbers you call most often?
- If you are an infrequent wireless consumer, consider a pre-paid cell

phone. I paid about $30 for a phone at Costco® and spend about $9 per month on mine. Can you beat that?

- If money is tight or you are looking for ways to boost savings, premium cable TV expense, in my opinion, is a potential goldmine for reclaiming cash. In the 30+ years since I moved out of my parents' house, I have never spent money on cable. A good old-fashioned antenna works just fine for the infrequent times that I want to watch something. Yes, I have missed out on plenty of reruns of *Gilligan's Island* and *The Brady Bunch*, darn it. On the other hand, my savings after 30 years is now into the tens of thousands of dollars and still counting. Do the math and decide. At a minimum, consider switching to basic cable.

Transportation

- **Alternatives to driving**: Walk, bicycle, or use public transit rather than a private vehicle if that's a viable option where you live. Monthly transit passes are a great deal if you use them frequently. Consider a car-share service like Zipcar® (**www.zipcar.com**) if there is one in your area.
- **New car purchase**: If you have your heart set on a new car, negotiate via the Internet. We solicited bids from four local dealers when we were shopping for our vehicles. There was quite a variation in the quotes. It was easy for us to get the lowest bid and not have the hassle of the traditional showroom haggling. Avoid options like spoilers, fancy wheels, keyless ignition and other things that don't help get you from point A to point B. These are profitable for the dealer. They don't have any functional value for you. Every $1,000 spent on stuff like that would have been worth about $25,000 in 40 years if invested instead. Remember that your shiny new set of wheels will just be a rusted hulk in 15 years and nearly worthless.
- **Car insurance**: At least every few years you should consider shopping around for the best insurance quote. Competitive prices can change significantly over time. If your vehicle is more than nine years old, check with your insurance agent to see whether it would make sense to drop the collision and comprehensive coverage. If the car gets wrecked at this age, its value might be so low that the insurance payout wouldn't be worth the expense.
- **Auto repair**: Consider using an independent AAA-approved shop rather than using the dealer. Research the shop at the Better Business Bureau (**www.bbb.org**) first.
- **Gasoline**: Find the least expensive gas in your area. A $0.15

reduction in the price per gallon saves the average driver about $100/year. Try **www.gasbuddy.com**. (Of course, don't drive your full-size SUV five miles out of your way just to get the cheaper gas. The savings will be eaten up.)

- **Overall vehicle expense**: The amount of money you can spend on vehicles in your lifetime is shocking. The next chapter on cars will show you how and why. Be sure to look there for other suggestions on how to save money on transportation.

Groceries

- **Grocery rewards programs**: Sign up for any rewards programs your favorite stores offer. They're free and membership entitles you to discounts, rebates, and special offers.
- **Coupons**: You may think this one's just for your Granny, but why not clip out the coupons that come in junk mail circulars or in the Sunday newspaper? You can also get online coupons from sites like **www.coupons.com**. It's free money they're offering, and if you're going to buy the stuff anyway, why not take the money? The Sunday newspaper coupons pay for my subscription and more. In addition, many large grocery chains are now offering online coupons that will upload directly to your store rewards card.
- **Generics**: Use the generic store brands where possible. Granted, some things you just don't compromise on. For me, one of those things is Charmin (enough said). However, there are many store brand items that contain exactly the same ingredients as the national brand, so there's no reason to pay more.
- **Stocking up**: If a non-perishable item goes on a big sale, back up the truck and fill up your storage shelves at home. As I mentioned before, I have about 30 boxes of our favorite cereals sitting in the garage. Every 3-4 months, they go on sale from $3.99 a box to $2.50 or so. I often have coupons as well, giving me a net price of around $1.50-$1.75. For our household, that's well over $200/year that stays in our pocket. Multiply this by the number of individual items you buy and you can see how quickly the savings add up.
- **Wine**: If you're of legal drinking age and you like to have a glass of wine at dinner, December is the best month to stock up on wine or champagne. Our favorite house wine is reliably offered at half-price that month, so we back up the truck and buy several months' supply. Our friends probably think we're winos when they see the collection of bottles

in storage. December is a prime month because lots of this stuff is consumed at holiday parties. The stores make up in volume what they lose in price, so everyone wins.

- **Prescription drugs**: Costco® and many large grocery chains now have pharmacies that offer generic prescription drugs at extremely favorable prices. Using mail order for your regular prescriptions may offer additional savings. Plus, you don't have to drive to the pharmacy each month to pick it up!

- **Know the price**: Get to know the usual prices on things you buy regularly. Comparison shop at a variety of stores and buy your favorites where they're cheapest. You'd be surprised the variation from store to store for the same item. There are also iPhone apps like RedLaser and ShopSavvy that allow you to scan a bar code. The app then shows you competing prices at several stores and online.

Other Retail

Negotiate: An establishment that does not post prices online or have a rate sheet for review is inviting you to negotiate. Health clubs and gyms are frequent perpetrators of this approach. Never take their first offer. For example, when we first enrolled in a local health club a few years ago, we told the sales associate we wanted her best deal. She gave us a price and said they could waive the $100 enrollment fee. We then said, "Our health insurer has discount agreements with several clubs. Do you participate?" We were then told that, yes, a 20% discount would be available. Ah. Better. We enrolled. Now fast forward a few years. We recently got a letter from the club informing us of a 38% dues increase from $69 to $95/month. That notice motivated us to shop around.

We found a competitor and met with the manager. "What's your best deal?" we said. He said they could offer $10/month discount on the second person and would also waive the enrollment fee. (It's funny how quickly the enrollment fee gets jettisoned with a customer who negotiates.) So the competitor's rate was $60 a month. Looking better, but we did not yet bite. After confirming that was his best offer, we thanked him and decided to poke around some more. We then discovered that Costco® was offering a two-year membership to a gym that worked out to $25/month total for the two of us. So, by switching clubs and using the Costco® deal we saved $1,680 over two years by not accepting the dues increase at our original club.

Price adjustment: If an item goes on sale after you've bought it, bring it back to the store with your receipt. Most stores will credit the difference if not too much time has elapsed.

Social media: Follow your favorite stores on Twitter or Facebook. Many retailers are beginning to use social media to pass along special deals.

Education: For those who see more education in their future, here are a few ideas to consider:

- Participate in tax-advantaged college savings plans and grant programs. We covered some of these in Chapter 5 ("*Uncle Sam*"). Here are two other websites you might review for locating scholarships and other information about funding your education: (1) **www.savingforcollege.com** and (2) **www.finaid.org**. Leave no stone unturned for free money!
- Plan to finish in no more than four years. Dawdling beyond that consumes fantastic quantities of tuition cash. If money is a serious obstacle, you might also consider a college that offers a three-year program. (Personally, I found the life experience of four years on campus so fantastic that I wouldn't trade it for anything. However, if there is just no other way to do it, be aware that the three-year option exists at some schools.)
- Buy your books used. Sell them back when you are finished.
- If there is no way you could afford a four-year college, consider community college for the first two years and then transfer. Community colleges are generally a very good value. Similarly, many public state schools are a relative bargain if you are an in-state student.

Travel

Welcome to my favorite category! My wife and I spend most of our discretionary money here. Happily, this is one of the biggest areas for obtaining discounts and avoiding fees, as long as you're paying attention and willing to do a little legwork. Here's why:

- Airlines and hotels are selling perishable products. An unsold airline seat generates exactly $0 in revenue for the air carrier. Once the flight departs, the possibility of income from empty seat 14A is lost forever. Similarly, a hotel room yields no cash if it's unoccupied overnight. Therefore, the companies have a strong incentive to make sure the seat/ room is occupied.
- Airlines and hotels are notorious for adding on additional fees in the hopes that their customers don't notice the full cost of their purchase. Here are some examples and estimated costs:
  - Airlines: Checked baggage fees ($25-50 per bag); charge for that crummy onboard meal ($5-10); headset fee ($5); charge for blanket ($5-10); fee to make any change to your ticket ($75 and up); frequent flyer award

ticket issue fee or "co-pay" ($50 and up); fee to book window or other desirable seats ($10 and up) ... and the list goes on.

○ Hotels: Internet access fees ($10-15/day); parking charge ($10-15/day); "resort fee" ($25); service charges for room service ... you get the idea.

One of my favorite hobbies is to defeat these companies at their own game. Let me show you how.

Hotels

For hotel bookings, I am a Priceline® evangelist. Nothing has come closer to satisfying my bargain-seeking instincts than their Name Your Own Price® service. Even though you won't know the name of the property in advance, if you select the "4-star" option there's a pretty good chance you won't end up at a dump. (We do like to travel in comfort. If you are less picky, you could select a hotel rating less than four stars. The procedure is the same.) I usually end up at national brand hotels and pay 40-50% below the best price available anywhere else. Here's how I do it:

- Browse prices on websites like Expedia® to get an idea of the going rate for the dates you want to stay. Also check individual hotel websites.
- Bring up Priceline.com® and find the Name Your Own Price® section. Enter the city and dates you want to stay and click "Bid Now." (Please note that you need to be 21 or older to use this service.)
- Notice that Priceline® has given you several "areas" within your desired destination unless it's a very small town/city. Click on each area one-by-one taking note at the bottom of the screen whether the neighborhood has a 4-star property. Create a list for those that have 4-star hotels and those that don't.
- Select the neighborhood with a 4-star property that is where you want to be. Enter an initial bid that is 50% less than the lowest-priced 4-star hotel that you browsed earlier. Fill in the information and press the button. If you get it, great!
- If your price is not accepted, here's the secret to rebidding. Priceline will not allow you to bid more than once in 24 hours unless you change something on your bid, like hotel "star level" or "area" in which you're willing to stay. Leave the original neighborhood and "4-star only" checked. Then, add one of the areas that did not have a 4-star property and increase your bid by $5-8. Since you know the area that you added does not have a 4-star hotel and you still have your desired neighborhood selected, you know you won't end up in the other neighborhood. This satisfies Priceline's requirement that you change something in your

bid in order to try again.

- If again you're unsuccessful, keep increasing the bid and adding other areas that don't have 4-star properties until the choices are exhausted. Try again 24 hours later at the price you left off if you strike out.

For hotels not booked on Priceline®, I try to find properties that don't have nuisance charges like parking, Internet, resort fees, etc. Poke around and see what fits with your lifestyle and budget.

If you are celebrating a special occasion like a birthday or anniversary, be sure to write a letter to the hotel's general manager in advance telling them so. I recommend formal, old-fashioned snail mail. You want them to know this is important and that you have put time and care into selecting their property. In the letter, I describe the reason we are coming and ask the manager to "please select a room appropriate for the occasion." We often get a nice upgrade and other amenities as a result. Special kudos to the Ritz-Carlton for upgrading us to an ocean-view suite with champagne, chocolate cake, and balloons on the occasion of my wife's 50th. I got serious brownie points for that one!

Airlines

- **Priceline®**: As much as I love Priceline® for hotel bookings, I have not used them for Name Your Own Price® airline tickets. The reason is that you could end up departing any time between 6 a.m. and 10 p.m. I have no interest in taking a chance on a red-eye flight at my age (been there, done that), especially when traveling with a seven-year-old. I also happen to despise certain airlines due to prior bad experiences. If you don't care about all that, give it a try! I'd consider using it myself on international flights, as these often are overnight trips anyway.
- **When to fly**: Avoid flying on Fridays and Sundays. These tend to be the most expensive days. Tuesday, Wednesday, and Thursday are often best, because demand is lower.
- **How and when to book flights**: Get a feeling for the lowest fares ever available for the routes you want to fly. For example, I know I'm doing pretty well when I see a roundtrip ticket for $100 (including all taxes) between San Diego and San Francisco. I start watching prices well in advance and when the price is right, I pounce. Don't dawdle—fares often appear and disappear quickly. If you like thrill seeking, this is a great game of chicken. The airline booking systems are constantly monitoring the number of seats booked versus historical averages. Their goal is to sell a seat for the greatest price, without leaving it empty at takeoff. Your

goal is to occupy that seat at the lowest price on the plane. Be patient. However, in my experience, once you get to within 14 days of your departure date, it's probably best to suck it up and buy the ticket. Fares generally are higher the closer you get to departure because the carriers soak business travelers who often need to travel on short notice and have no flexibility in their schedule.

- **Southwest Airlines**: There's only one domestic airline I've flown that does not charge any of the ridiculous fees shown above (at least as of this writing), and that's Southwest Airlines. I love them. They charge reasonable fares, they have none of the stupid fees, they're generally nice to customers, and their on-time record is pretty good.
- **Credit vouchers**: If you notice a significant price drop after buying your ticket, call the airline and see if they'll issue a "travel credit voucher" for the difference. It's not as good as getting your money back, but at least you'll have a credit to use on a future flight. On Southwest Airlines, they will "bank" the difference for you for a full year with no fee.
- **Luggage**: Pack so that your luggage fits in an approved carry-on suitcase. Never check a bag, especially if your airline charges a fee. Experienced business travelers always travel this way and so should you. Not only do you save on the baggage fee, but you know your bag will arrive with you. You also save time upon arrival.
- **Meals in the air**: Bring your own food with you. It'll be tastier, healthier, and cheaper than any food service offered by the airline (if they offer food at all).

Rental Cars

- Many car rental companies won't rent to people under the age of 25. If their policies allow rentals to younger drivers, often they'll charge an additional (and hefty) "Young Renter" fee. Call them ahead of time to determine their requirements and fees.
- "Weekend" rentals (usually noon Thursday through noon Monday) are often much cheaper than mid-week.
- Try Priceline's Name Your Own Price® service.
- Insurance: This is one of the rental car industry's contributions to the overinflated fee syndrome. Before accepting any insurance that they offer, make sure you've contacted your own auto insurance company ahead of time to see if you're already covered for rental car use. Be sure you are clear on what your own car insurance will cover or not cover on a rented vehicle before you decide to accept or decline the insurance offered by

the car rental company. You may still want to accept their coverage if there is a significant gap between your own policy coverage and that offered by the car rental firm.

- Some rental car companies get a bit sneaky by charging an inexpensive daily rate to get your attention. Then, they charge you an additional fee for every mile you drive! Read the fine print in the contract. Make sure the company gives you unlimited miles or a quantity sufficient to cover the driving you will do.
- City hotels often charge a fortune to park on their property overnight. (In San Francisco, I've seen prices as high as $60/night.) Better to use public transit if possible. Rent a car for longer day trips and return it before you get back to the hotel.

Eating While Traveling

- Dining out in a new city is one of the joys of travel. See elsewhere in this chapter for advice on eating well for a good price.
- Eat like the locals. For example, in Italy we paid as much for a bottle of wine as we did for a small can of soda. Lesson: skip the soda in Italy. Get restaurant recommendations from local people and avoid places frequented by tourists. The food is generally better and the prices are more favorable.
- When traveling, we tend to be most interested in a dinner adventure and don't care much about breakfast and lunch. For those meals, we'll often visit a local supermarket to pick up groceries. Supermarket delis are great places to get a good sandwich for a reasonable cost and tips are not expected!

Other Helpful Travel Services and Tips

- **Expedia.com® and Travelocity.com®**: These are wonderful online booking systems for flights, hotels, cars, and cruises that often offer some good deals.
- **Bing™ from Microsoft (www.bing.com/travel)**: These guys have some interesting technology that tells you whether current prices are a good deal relative to historical prices. They can also help you monitor flight routes and give you advice on whether it's a good time to buy.
- **Southwest's Ding!® service**: Download "Ding!" from Southwest Airlines (www.southwest.com/ding), which will give you several daily specials not available anywhere else. I've occasionally received fabulous deals

from this program.

- **International travel**: Check with your bank or credit union to see if they charge fees to convert foreign currency transactions back to U.S. dollars when you use a credit card or debit/ATM card. (Yes, those sneaky banks never miss an opportunity to gouge you.) If they do, get a different card that doesn't charge these fees. To obtain cash in the local currency, we've found that using your ATM card at foreign banks usually gives a better exchange rate than the retail services you'll find at airports or downtown.

- **Social media**: Follow your favorite travel companies on Twitter or Facebook, as many have begun using social media to communicate special deals.

- **Travelzoo®** (www.travelzoo.com): Subscribe to Travelzoo's newsletter. It is also a good source for current travel deals.

- **Airport transit**: Have a friend drop you off or use public transit if available. A shuttle service or shared taxi is the next best choice. Solo taxi or on-site airport parking can be quite expensive.

Entertainment

- Buy an Entertainment® book from one of the many local non-profits that sell them or at **www.entertainment.com**. Available for many metro areas, these books offer huge discounts on dining, entertainment, hotels, museums, and the like. You should be able to save more than you spent for the book with little effort.

- Take advantage of free entertainment in your local area (concerts, parks, museums, lectures, etc.). Many museums in our area, for example, have one day a month where they offer free admission.

- Movies and theatre: Go to matinees. Use discount coupons from the Entertainment® book. Warehouse clubs like Costco® often sell reduced price tickets. Join movie theater clubs for discounts.

Dining Out

- Look for coupons in the junk mail circulars that show up in your mailbox.
- Check the restaurant's website for special deals, such as happy hours, half-price wine nights, and so on.
- Use Restaurant.com® (**www.restaurant.com**) to buy greatly discounted restaurant gift cards.
- Enroll with OpenTable® (**www.opentable.com**). Not only can you make online reservations for free, they offer a "Dining Rewards" program that

lets you accrue points toward dining gift certificates. Look for the "1,000 point" deals, which are worth ten times the usual reward value.

- Order appetizers rather than an entrée or share an entrée with your date. Better for the waistline too!
- If you like wine with a meal, you've probably noticed that alcohol has a very high markup at restaurants. Rather than paying inflated prices, bring your own bottle to places that have a low corkage fee.
- During the holiday season, many of the restaurants in our area offer gift cards at a discount. ("Buy a $50 card for only $35!") We not only buy some to give as gifts, we buy extra from our favorite places and keep them for ourselves to use throughout the year.

Miscellaneous

Workplace lunches: Bring your lunch to work rather than buying at the cafeteria or going out. If you're a coffee drinker, bring your own in a travel mug. Assuming a $6/day savings, these steps alone will save you more than $1,500/year.

Smoking: If you're looking for one more bit of motivation to quit, let me point out that money spent on a moderate (or heavy) smoking habit may fully fund your retirement if redirected to your investment account instead. I wish you success in this.

The beverage bonanza: I have a friend from Spain who marvels at the success that American beverage companies have had marketing sugar water to billions of people around the world and making fabulous profits doing it. Check out the contents of most soda cans and you will see, indeed, that the stuff is mostly comprised of water and sugar (or artificial sweetener if a diet beverage). Bottled water falls into a similar category. Beverage companies created a need that people didn't know they had and then convinced us to spend lots of money on it.

Bottom line: Unless you live next to a toxic-waste dump, consume good old-fashioned municipal tap water and forget the soda and bottled water. Buy a BPA-free water bottle and refill it while you're on the go.

While you're at it, keep a careful eye on your fancy coffee habit. I happen to love cappuccinos. The daily jolt to my wallet eventually persuaded me to severely limit my intake. My wife and I saved over $100 per month when we deleted soda, bottled water, and cappuccinos. (And we feel healthier!) I'd encourage you to do the math for yourself if you are an avid consumer of any of the products in this category—you might be shocked!

Books and movies: Use your local library. Get access to a huge selection of books, videos/DVDs, and music for free!

Beauty products and hair: I realize I may be venturing into dangerous territory with you ladies on this one. I'm talking about hair. I won't even touch highlights, manicures, polish, and that sort of stuff. (Personally, I think you're all beautiful without all that goop.) I'll just stick to haircuts. In fact, I'll even just direct this to the guys to keep myself out of trouble.

I pay $7 for a haircut. In San Francisco, one of the most expensive cities in the country, I used to pay $5 at a Chinatown barbershop. Why anyone would pay more is beyond me. The darn stuff just grows back in a few weeks so why worry about it? Maybe I'm wrong and people are just being polite, but I don't think anyone would guess I pay $7 when they look at my finely trimmed graying head. Except now my secret's out ... "Hey check out that guy over there with the $7 haircut. Isn't he the one that wrote that book?" Sigh.

Designer clothing: I continue to marvel at the fashion industry's success in selling apparel that is marked up many times over the cost of the material and labor required to produce the item. That $80 designer shirt/blouse or $150 pants likely consist of about $5 in labor and material. The rest is mostly marketing (you have to pay those celebrities a lot of money to endorse a product), a bit of overhead expense, and profits for all the players. When your high-end department store holds one of its regular "Super Sales," do you think they are losing money on everything they sell? No way. That's how high the markups can be.

Over the last few years, my wife has converted from the high-end department stores and is happy to report that stores like Ross, Marshall's and Kohl's reliably meet her fashion requirements at much better prices. Try factory outlet or overstock stores that sell the same designer clothes at lower prices. Consignment or "new to you" stores might also be worth a look. At a minimum, avoid fashions that are so trendy that they can't be worn for at least a couple of seasons. And of course, never pay full retail price, right? Also, consider buying clothes that don't require dry cleaning to eliminate that expense.

Resole shoes: This is way cheaper than buying new ones. And you won't have to break them in again!

This Is Just a Sampling ...

I've just done a brain dump of everything I could think of that might offer you opportunities to save money on common purchases. I am sure that once the book goes to press I will think of others. So will you. That is why Principle #3 (*"Distinguish between wants and needs"*) and Principle #4 (*"Never pay full retail"*) must be deeply ingrained when managing your spending.

We are fortunate to live in a country where there is such an abundance of products to make our lives easier and more fun. At the same time, the choices can be overwhelming. Advertising firms are good at compelling us to buy products we don't really need. Corporations try to convince us to buy stuff at prices that may not be the best value available in the marketplace. As consumers, we need to be just as clever as those pitching their products at us. It all boils down to three simple questions:

1. Do I really need the product I am looking at?
2. If no and I still want it, does it fit in my budget?
3. Where can I get the best price if I decide to buy?

CHAPTER 7

The $6,745,171 Automobile Collection

"Get a bicycle. You will not regret it. If you live."
— MARK TWAIN

Buying a house will likely be the biggest purchase in your life. The second largest, I'm guessing, will be the happy day you procure a new set of wheels. Maybe you've already made the leap into car ownership. Perhaps you're still waiting to enter the club. Either way, I thought it would be worthwhile to devote a chapter to this subject so that you have a chance to fully understand the amount of cash being vacuumed out of your bank account by your beautiful piece of freedom on wheels.

For the last several decades, one of the great rites of passage for American teenagers has been to get their own car. Finally freed from their parents' boring mini-vans, they're on the road to freedom, adventure, and with luck, a little hanky-panky in the backseat.

The advertising firms from Madison Avenue and the Hollywood film-makers have all done their part to create an image that hot cars get the girls (or boys, depending); horsepower and muscle are good; and you're not cool if you don't have a sexy car. From what I can tell, guys seem to be most suscep-tible to this for some reason. (Why do the car ads always have some sexy babe conspicuously placed in the scenery?)

Many of us have bought into this idea in one way or another. While the advertising message changes a bit as you get older ("Our mini-van/SUV is the safest vehicle for your family"), it's the same idea. They tell you that if you get a new car every three or four years, your life will be great.

So here comes the math geek to spoil the fun. What if I told you that, over a driving lifetime, your car obsession can cost you millions of dollars?

I'll use the automobile expense category as a way to illustrate the time value of money and compound interest concepts we discussed earlier. A quick note to you mathematical purists: I will probably annoy you with the lack of precision in some of this. Please bear with me. For example, I realize that a 10-year-old car may have some residual trade-in value that may slightly change the results posted here. I'm trying to keep this simple to illustrate the point.

Running the Numbers

Let's make the following assumptions:

- You are 21 years old and plan to drive for 54 years.
- Every three years, you want to get rid of your current vehicle and drive a new one.
- You haven't saved much money, so you don't have a lot of cash to put down.
- You decide to lease the vehicle each time you acquire one. You'll have a lease for three years and at the end of the lease period, you give the car back to the dealer. (With leasing, you essentially are renting the car for an extended period. You do not own it.) At the end of the lease, you pick out another cool car and sign a lease for another three years. And so on.
- Let's assume a lease price of roughly $350 a month, which would include the lease cost, sales tax, and the "amount due at signing" spread out over the life of the lease. This amount is my best estimate for a vehicle with a listed retail price of about $19,000. Dealers may occasionally offer promotional deals for well-qualified buyers that might be less than this. (After we go through the entire process you will be equipped to run the numbers for the exact vehicle you have your eye on.)
- To keep this easy, we'll also assume that every time you lease another car the lease price stays at $350 a month. In the real world, the lease price is likely to go up over time due to inflation.

So, by the time you get to age 75, you will have leased 18 cars. Your payments over a driving lifetime come out to $226,800. Sounds high, don't you think? Well, it gets worse. Our calculation so far neglects the **opportunity cost** of the money you spent on the leases. Opportunity cost in this instance simply refers to the money you could have made by investing that money elsewhere. Rather than leasing cars over 54 years, if you had instead invested the same amount in the stock market with a hypothetical 8% per year annual return, you would have $3,838,715 in your brokerage account at the end.

You may now pick your jaw up off the floor because we're not done yet. Missing from the picture is a bunch of other expenses associated with our awesome hunk of metallic sex appeal. Let's add in the following items:

- **Maintenance**: Oil changes, replacement tires, and other regularly scheduled service appointments add up. Let's figure about $50 per month for this stuff.
- **Registration fees**: In the fine state of California where I live, this can be a fairly hefty fee. I recently paid $221 to register my three-year-old Honda Civic. Your state could be more or less. Let's assume $20 per month.

- **Gasoline**: This is a big one, which we'll discuss in more detail later. For now, let's say you drive 12,000 miles per year and your buggy gets 20 miles per gallon. That's 600 gallons a year. It's hard to predict gas prices since they fluctuate so much. Humor me here and accept a working amount of $2.75 per gallon. This comes to about $135 per month.
- **Insurance**: Another whopper, especially if you're young. I'm in the "older than age 25" category with no accidents or moving violations (a dream customer for the insurance company). Insurance for my trusty 2006 Honda Civic is about $700 per year. So let's use $60 per month for insurance because we know you're a great driver too. (Honestly, this number is likely too low if you are under 25. In the unlikely event you're not a dream customer for the insurance company, this number will be MUCH higher, especially if you're male and under age 25. Sorry, dudes.)

The add-ons we just included come to $265 every month. Here is where we are now:

- Lease cost: $350 monthly
- Maintenance, insurance, gas, registration: $265 monthly
- Total monthly = $615
- Expense over 54 years = $398,520

As before, had you invested that $615/month instead, at age 75 your brokerage account balance would have been

$6,745,171

How's that for an eye-popping number? Wouldn't you like to have that amount at your disposal when you're done working? When you own a house, at least you have a decent chance that it will eventually be worth more than you paid for it. Your beautiful vehicle, however, nearly always depreciates to be practically worthless after 15 years or so. All the money you spend on a car goes out the door and doesn't come back.

At this point you may be thinking, "Ok, I get that cars are expensive, but I need to get around somehow and public transit isn't a great option where I live." Fair enough. Let's look at some alternatives that might drive our seven-figure number down a bit.

Fuel Efficiency

Let's take the same example but change the vehicle's mileage to 40 mpg rather than 20. Yes, there are several cars available now that get that kind of mileage with many more on the way. (By the way, if you are driving a full-size SUV, your mileage is probably worse than the 20 mpg I used earlier. Factor this in accordingly.) Using 40 mpg as our fuel efficiency number drops gallons burned annually from 600 to 300, a savings of $825 ($68.75/month). Over your hypothetical driving lifetime, this results in a savings of $44,550 or a balance of $754,033 if invested rather than spent. We've just lopped off about 11% of our automobile ownership expense.

Fuel-efficient vehicles do have one drawback you will want to ponder. Cars that get great mileage tend to be smaller vehicles. In the event of a collision with a truck or large SUV, the laws of physics will not favor the lighter vehicle. An extra investment in safety options is well worth it—in any vehicle, for that matter. For that reason, we made sure to get the optional side curtain air bags on both our Toyota Prius and Honda Civic. Front seat driver and passenger air bags were standard equipment. When you are shopping, be sure to research the crash safety ratings of the vehicles you have under consideration.

If you want the extra bulk of a larger vehicle for safety or lifestyle choices, there is still a wide range of fuel efficiency choices on the market. You could buy a 30 mpg SUV, for example, rather than a 15 mpg vehicle and still see a 50% reduction in your fuel consumption to achieve financial savings similar to those outlined above.

By the way, when you purchase a fuel-efficient vehicle, you get more than just the financial benefits outlined above. A higher mileage vehicle does some other nice things:

1. Consuming less gasoline results in lower petroleum imports to the United States. Many oil-exporting countries are not particularly fond of the USA; some are actively trying to harm us. Why would we as a nation want to continue to fill the coffers of people like this? High mileage cars can help us reduce our dependence on foreign oil.
2. Burning gasoline dumps carbon dioxide into the earth's atmosphere, contributing to global warming. Vehicles that consume less fuel do less damage to Mother Earth.

My Adventures With "Pre-Owned" Cars

I am not a big fan of auto leasing. You shell out a big pile of money for three or four years, then you return the car to the dealer and have nothing to show for it. I'd rather pay cash and drive a car until it falls apart. (Or in the case of my trusty 12-year-old Toyota Celica, until a San Francisco taxicab runs a stop sign and totals it.)

My brother is even more frugal than I am. He's a corporate treasurer for a large software company who still drives his wife's 17-year-old Toyota Tercel to work every day. I can only wonder what his outside corporate bankers think when he takes them to lunch. As the car gets older and looks more decrepit, my brother takes it as a matter of pride that the little buggy is still running. So you can see what's in my DNA.

My first foray into the world of used cars was a 1969 Buick Wildcat that I bought for $300 in 1981. The Wildcat was classic Detroit Big Iron. It had one of the biggest V8 engines GM ever made that gulped fuel at a rate of 8 mpg. It was a bowl of jelly on wheels with a trunk so big my roommates were convinced I could fit the entire naval Fifth Fleet inside it in a pinch. The radio antenna had broken off, so I used a coat hanger in its place.

Sadly, the darn thing was always breaking down on me. I had a 15-mile "radius of confidence", meaning that I wouldn't drive it any farther than that for fear it would leave me stranded somewhere. So, I ended up taking public transit to work most of the time, which actually worked out fine. I saved a bunch of money I would have spent on a car. My big lesson, though, was never buy a car that makes you bust out laughing when you first set eyes on it.

My second used car experience wasn't much better. In 1982, I purchased a 1973 Toyota Corolla for about $1,200. A couple months after I bought it, the engine was losing functional cylinders one by one. This is a particularly big problem in a car with only four cylinders. It would literally take 60 seconds to get up to full speed on the freeway. In a regular morning ritual, my housemates would gather at the bottom of our hilly driveway to see whether my car would muster enough energy to get itself up the hill and out to the street. If it didn't, they'd all band together and help push it up the hill. I'm a slow learner, but what I eventually figured out was this: unless you're a gear head who likes working on cars, avoid vehicles that are greater than 10 years old at the time of purchase.

Consider a "Gently Used" Car

I hope I haven't completely scared you away from used cars with my earlier stories. In retrospect, I got what I paid for considering the age of the vehicles I bought. A recent-model gently used car could be a very good choice, if you buy a model with a reputation for quality and reliability. In fact, this is where I finally had some success with a used car. After the San Francisco cabbie wrecked my Toyota Celica, I bought a six-year-old Lexus from a co-worker. I paid $15,000 cash, which was easily half the original cost and I got another seven years of relatively trouble-free life out of it.

Consider buying something that's three or four years old, as cars tend to lose most of their value in those first years. Yet, they should still have many years of good life on them. For example, I paid $17,200 for a new Honda Civic in 2006. If I sold it today in a private party transaction, it would be worth less than $12,000 four years later.

So let's pull a pencil out of the pocket protector and update our numbers with the "gently used car" scenario. Here are our assumptions:

- Beginning at age 21 you'll buy a four-year-old car that gets 40 mpg. You'll drive it for seven years, repeating every seven years until age 75. You will buy eight cars during this time.
- Assume a purchase price of $12,000 in today's dollars, including sales tax. If each car lasts seven years, this works out to about $143/month[7]. Since you're driving an older vehicle, you'll need to add in extra maintenance expenses. Let's estimate an extra $30/month over the life of the car when compared with our earlier leasing example.
- The purchase cost works out to $143/month. Maintenance, registration, insurance, and fuel are another $197. Add $30 extra maintenance expense and you arrive at $227/month. (Note that I've reduced the fuel expense by $68 per month over the leasing example because your vehicle is getting 40 mpg rather than 20.) Total monthly expense is $143 + $227 = $370.
- Lifetime cash spent on your vehicles in this scenario: $370/month x 12 months/year x 54 years = $239,760. As before, had we invested the same amount at 8% over 54 years, you would have had $4,058,070 in the bank instead.

---

[7] *If you financed the car at 5% interest over 48 months, then the acquisition cost rises from $143/ month to $158/month ($15/month additional) when spread out over seven years.*

Let's look at how this compares with our earlier leasing scenario:

	Monthly Outlay	Cash Paid Out Over 54 Years	Opportunity Cost
Lease every 3 years; 20 mpg	$615	$398,520	$6,745,171
Buy used every 7 years; 40 mpg	$370	$239,760	$4,058,070
Savings	$245	$158,760	$2,687,101

By obtaining a used vehicle every seven years and getting better gas mileage, you save $2.7 million over a driving lifetime when compared with our leasing example.

I Really Want to Buy a Brand New Car!

The last option to consider is the purchase of a new vehicle. How does that compare financially? Let's look at the same $19,000 vehicle that we evaluated in the leasing example. We'll assume you have no money to put down and finance the entire purchase at 2% interest over 48 months. You live in California and pay about 8.5% sales tax. We will spread out the sales tax over 48 months to arrive at a monthly number. Your monthly payment would be $412, plus $33 tax = $445 per month over four years.

The good news in this example is that the car would be yours after the payments end, unlike the lease where you return the car to the dealer at the end of the contract.

Let's compare the new car acquisition expense versus the used and lease examples. To get an apples-to-apples comparison, we will assume that you financed the $12,000 used car at an interest rate of 5% over 48 months[8]. The monthly payment for the used car comes out to $276, including tax. Compare this with $445 for the new car and $350 in the leasing example.

[8.] *Interest rates on used cars are generally a bit higher than new cars. As in the earlier used car example, I have also assumed that sales tax is included in the $12,000 price.*

Acquisition Cost Comparison
(Excludes Gas, Insurance, Maintenance, Registration, Etc.)

	Monthly Payment Years 1-4	Monthly Payment Years 5-7	Average Payment Over 7 Years
Lease every 3 years	$350	$350	$350
Buy new, keep for 7 years	$445	▸$0	$254
Buy used, keep for 7 years	$276	$0	$158

Other Variations

We've been cranking away with the calculator for a while now, so I won't throw any more numbers at you. However, on your own, I'd encourage you to experiment with other variations to arrive at a scenario that's optimal for your life. Examples include:

- Buy a new or used car with cash and keep it until it dies.
- Add in financing expense if you can't pay cash.
- If you do pay cash, evaluate the opportunity cost of using the money to buy a car versus investing that money elsewhere.
- Own the vehicles for a longer period (12 years? 15 years?).
- Adjust the fuel expense.
- Vary the initial cost of the vehicle. For example, if you're pining for a hot German sports car, your acquisition cost will likely be much higher than our earlier examples.

If you are a math geek and want to run precise scenarios on your own, get a financial calculator like an HP12C to help you. No matter how you look at it, owning an automobile is an extremely expensive proposition over your lifetime.

Whatever you do, don't take the path I took with my first new car purchase way back in 1984. This was the Toyota Celica GT that we talked about earlier. Remember that I was still clueless about managing my money at that time. I took out a 100% loan at 12% interest and put the tax and license fees on my credit card at 18%. I still cringe when I think back about how stupid that was. But hey, it was a chick magnet, right?

A Few Final Thoughts On Personal Transportation

I'd encourage you to think differently than my generation has about how we get around. If public transit is a viable option where you live, please consider it. Is walking a good choice? Cycling? Some cities have car sharing services like Zipcar® (**www.zipcar.com**) for occasional car needs. Don't reflexively buy a car because TV ads and society says you need to have one to be cool.

Here's the bottom line for the guys out there. If you want to be a chick magnet for superficial reasons, I can assure you that in 10 years most women will be more impressed with the size of your bank account rather than the size of your ... car engine.

If you want to have $1,000,000 in your pocket at age 65, one of the easiest ways to get there is to minimize your personal transportation expense and invest the savings. Next to housing, transportation could easily be one of your biggest expenses—and much of it is discretionary.

As we've seen in this chapter, buying a gently used car with minimal add-ons and driving it for many years costs much less than buying or leasing a new vehicle every three or four years.

You'll save a bundle if you can forego the expense of owning your own car. You'll also do Mother Nature a favor by reducing pollution and carbon dioxide emissions that contribute to global warming.

Given where you live, perhaps a personal vehicle is the only option. If so, that's fine. Just be sure you've really thought about it and have evaluated alternatives. End of sermon. Now go out and buy your Hummer.

CHAPTER 8

Home, Sweet Home?

"There is no place more delightful than one's own fireside."
— CICERO

As with automobiles, home ownership is one of those "American as apple pie" ideals. How often have you heard that owning a house is the American dream? In many ways it has been a great thing for millions of families since World War II. However, residential real estate prices got out of hand in the first decade of the 21st century. Many people bought houses during an explosive real estate bubble with little money down and with mortgages they didn't understand. They considered their new properties "investments" that would always go up in value.

This went on happily for several years until the game of musical chairs came to a most unpleasant end in 2007-2008. Housing prices then declined nationally during that period and many people found themselves owing more money on their house than the place was worth.

When the party ended, many lost their houses to foreclosure or simply walked away, which in turn affected the rest of us who were prudent. How so, you may ask?

- Foreclosed homes are often in bad condition, so buyers offer a lot less money for them. Even if the places are in good condition, banks are eager to get them off their books, so they're often sold at low prices. This drives down prices for surrounding homes in the neighborhood.
- The federal government has spent hundreds of billions of dollars bailing out the banks that issued the bad mortgages and the buyers who assumed them. That money eventually will need to be paid back by you and me, the United States taxpayer. Sadly for you and your peers, much of the debt the government took on to do this will fall on your generation to repay.

Even before the recent debacle, so many people considered their homes a great investment it was just assumed that this was so. In my 25 years of owning various houses, I've yet to have the experience of my home being a "great investment." Yes, home ownership offers personal satisfaction and frees you from dealing with a landlord. At the same time, owning a house sucks a lot of money out of your pocket and generally needs to be a fairly long-term commitment to come out ahead financially.

The purpose of this chapter, therefore, is to show you the pros and cons of buying a house versus renting so that you can decide which is most appropriate for you. My brother the corporate treasurer has never owned a house because he's convinced that his cash will return more money if invested elsewhere. (The cost of renting in his area and mine is much lower than buying.)

I completely agree with his intellectual arguments on the cash. For me, the emotional draw of owning won out. If you decide to buy at the end of all this, that's great! If not, that's great! Either way, the stuff we'll discuss in the coming pages will help you go into this decision with your eyes wide open.

Before I take you through the details, we'll need to cover some basic definitions:

- **Principal and interest**: Principal is the amount you're borrowing. Interest is the extra money you're paying the bank for the privilege of using their money.
- **Down payment**: This is the amount of your own money that you must provide at the time of purchase. Lenders typically look for at least 10%. However, 20% is better. (See PMI below.)
- **Mortgage loan**: This is debt owed to a lender (bank, credit union, or other entity) when you purchase a home. The loan is secured by the property, which means that if you don't pay the amounts due in a timely fashion, the bank can take your house. There are many flavors of mortgages. The basic ones are:
  - **30-year fixed** rate: You pay a fixed monthly amount (principal and interest) for 30 years and then the loan is completely paid off.
  - **15-year fixed** rate: Same thing, but the loan is paid in 15 years. Typically, this type of loan has an interest rate that is about 0.5% lower than a 30-year mortgage.
  - **Adjustable rate mortgage (ARM)**: A mortgage whose monthly payment varies according to a pre-determined formula, typically based on an underlying index like the one-year Treasury bond rate. These can be useful in an environment when interest rates are expected to come down over a very long period. If interest rates come down, your monthly payment drops. However, the opposite happens when interest rates are rising. Some people also use them to get into a bigger house than they could otherwise afford because they expect their salary to continue rising. (My opinion: using an ARM in that way is risky.)
  - **Conforming mortgage**: This is a loan that "conforms" to requirements specified by government-sponsored finance entities. One of the key requirements is the maximum loan amount. I wish I could just give you a number, but it is not that simple. The conforming loan amounts vary

by location. (Go to **www.fanniemae.com** for the latest information.) The key thing to know is that a conforming mortgage typically has an interest rate that is less than a "non-conforming" mortgage (which is sometimes called a **jumbo loan**). At some point in your future you may purchase a gigantic mansion (or a hovel in Newport Beach) that requires a jumbo loan. Until that point, don't worry about it.

- ○ **Private Mortgage Insurance (PMI)**: An insurance policy that pays the bank what they're owed in the event you default (stop paying) on your mortgage loan. This will typically be required if your down payment is less than 20%. The buyer pays all costs for this. (How about that! The bank makes you pay for an insurance policy that benefits them if you don't pay the mortgage! I think I want to be a banker in my next life.) PMI can be dropped once the owner's equity in the house reaches 20%, either through property appreciation or by paying down principal.

- **Points and fees**: Points are, in effect, prepaid interest to the bank payable at the time you originate the loan. So one "point" means you pay one percent of the loan amount up front. On a $200,000 loan, that's a quick $2,000 out of your pocket.

  - ○ Some banks push points because in return, they say, "We'll lower your interest rate and therefore your monthly payments if you pay points." This is fine if you'll be in your house for a very long time or if you never plan to refinance. Most people either refinance from time to time or don't stay in the house long enough to make it up, so the bank often ends up the winner if you opt to pay points.

  - ○ Once again, a financial calculator can be a big help in looking at the tradeoffs. Alternately, you could ask the lender to show you the numbers for multiple scenarios so that you can properly assess the best way to go. Since a bank never misses an opportunity to squeeze out a few extra bucks, most lenders will also attach a variety of fees to your loan. These fees must be disclosed to you.

- **Refinance**: This refers to the process of closing out an existing mortgage and replacing it with one that is (hopefully) more favorable to you. People typically refinance when interest rates have dropped enough to result in lower payments. Refinancing usually involves various costs and fees, so the monthly payments need to drop enough to outweigh the costs of refinancing. Be aware that when you refinance, the mortgage payoff date also resets. For example, if you have been paying on a 30-year loan for five years and then refinance, the new 30-year loan will be retired in 30 years, not 25 years (assuming you refinanced to another 30-year loan).

- **Negative amortization**: Some mortgages have features that allow you to pay a below-market interest rate for a while or make a smaller payment. In return, the bank adds on principal to your balance. If this happens, you can end up owing more than you borrowed! In my opinion, you should NEVER take out a loan with this feature.
- **Pre-payment penalty**: This is another sneaky way for banks to gouge you. This clause says that if you pay off the loan before some pre-determined period of time, you owe the bank a sizable fee. You may want to prepay if you want to refinance or sell your house, so avoid loans like this.
- **Property tax**: Local and/or state governments generally levy an annual tax on your property that varies from roughly 1-3% of the property's assessed value. Every jurisdiction calculates this differently. In California where I live, you'd pay roughly $6,000 per year for your property tax if the house were assessed at $500,000. You'll need to budget for this big chunk of change.
- **Homeowners insurance**: Required by your lender to cover against various risks to your property like fire, theft, and so on. (Even if you owned your home free and clear you'd want to have this protection.) Have discussions with several insurance agents to determine what is most appropriate for your situation and geographic area. Try different deductibles (the amount you're responsible for before the insurance company pays out) to see how this affects the price. Add the quoted amount to your budget.
- **Homeowners Association (HOA)**: Some housing communities and most condominium complexes are subject to oversight by an HOA. The HOA is responsible for maintenance of the community's common areas and enforcement of the "Covenants, Conditions, and Restrictions" (also called CC&Rs). CC&Rs are the community rules and restrictions that you'll need to read before you buy, and then follow once you become a member of the community. Read carefully before you buy. For example, if you're a gear head who likes to work on your car in the driveway, many communities governed by CC&Rs prohibit that kind of activity. In this example, you might not want to live in a place like that. An HOA generally assesses a monthly fee to each owner. This can range from a small amount to several hundred dollars a month. Budget accordingly.

Now that we've covered some basic definitions, let's return to our analysis of home ownership expenses. To do this, we'll use a real-life example. My family and I live in a typical Southern California suburban house on a puny lot that we bought for $525,000 in 2002. (For those of you living in locations where the typical house costs $150,000, don't be too impressed. Our house is not a McMansion. This is what it costs to live in sunny California.) After being in the home for nearly eight years, here is a brief tally of the expenses we've incurred to date:

Item	Cost
Initial purchase price	$525,000
• Kitchen remodel	25,000
• Termite tenting	3,000
• Dry rot/termite repairs for decks and patio trellis	15,000
• Energy efficient windows and doors	9,000
• Solar electric system	13,000
• Paint house (soon)	7,000
• Insurance	13,000
• Property tax	45,000
• Homeowners Association fees	18,000
• Miscellaneous repairs and maintenance	5,000
ADJUSTED "COST" (Purchase price + expenses)	**$678,000**

If we had a typical mortgage (30-year loan with 20% down), we would have paid well over $150,000 in interest expense during the same period, bringing the total outlay to over $825,000.

We were fortunate to have purchased before the huge run up in prices from 2002-2007. Similar houses in our neighborhood rose to $785,000 at the peak. As of mid-2010, the latest comparable sales price is $620,000. If we had to sell now, we'd pay 6% in realtor commissions and other fees, leaving us with a net price of $582,800, assuming we received a similar sale price. After several years of living here, our total cost is $678,000 (excluding mortgage expense, which we don't have). So, we are currently sitting on a loss approaching $100,000. What a great investment! Yes, if we sit tight for several more years we will hopefully recoup that loss and then some, but you get the idea.

The analysis up to now is incomplete because we have neglected to consider a very real benefit of home ownership, and that is rent avoidance. Clearly, money you're paying out to rent is permanently lost, yet you need to have a place to live. So, let's now compare the cost of owning this house with the expense of renting a similar place in my neighborhood, which is currently about $3,000 per month. We'll assume a purchase price of $620,000, since that is the latest comparable price. We'll also apply a 20% down payment, and a 30-year mortgage at 5.5% interest. Our monthly cost of owning the house can be described as follows:

Item	Monthly Cost
Mortgage	$2,816
HOA dues	$200
Homeowners and earthquake insurance	$150
Property tax	$620
Repair and maintenance expense	$300
Capital improvements (new kitchen, solar system, etc) spread out over 20 years	$160
TOTAL	**$4,246**

There's one more thing to consider in this analysis and that is the benefit of the tax deduction for mortgage interest and property tax that is available for your personal residence. (Refer back to the chapter on Uncle Sam for a detailed discussion of this.) The exact value of this benefit is dependent upon:

1. Your federal and state marginal tax brackets.
2. The degree to which the mortgage and property tax expense (and other non-housing deductions) exceeds your standard deduction, allowing you to itemize.

Let's continue with the same example and assume that you are in the 25% marginal federal tax bracket and 8% state bracket. We'll also assume that you are already itemizing your deductions. We'll estimate your mortgage interest deduction to be worth about $2,200/month[9]. The deductible property tax is $620/month. The total tax-deductible amount is $2,820/month ($2,200+$620). How does the cost of buying versus renting now compare?

---

[9] In the early years, most of your mortgage payment is interest. Yes, the bank gets their interest before you get your equity.

Monthly After-Tax Ownership Expense Versus Renting

Total cost of owning	$4,246
Less federal tax benefit ($2,820 x .25)	-$705
Less state tax benefit ($2,820 x .08)	-$226
Monthly after-tax ownership expense	**$3,315**
Monthly cost to rent similar house	$3,000
Additional monthly cost to own	**$315**

In this example, the monthly outlay for owning is approaching the cost of renting when you factor in the tax savings. (The tax benefit here is $931/month.) The bad news is that the cash you used for your $124,000 down payment is no longer available to earn interest or grow long-term in the stock market.

You would want to do a more precise analysis for your specific situation before you decide to buy. Using your trusty financial calculator (or your trusty accountant) and the information here, you should now have the tools to do this.

After reviewing all the details we've covered here, I hope you can see that a house purchase might be a good investment and it might not. You can improve your odds if you: (1) own the place a very long time (more than 10 years); (2) don't overpay in a hot market; and (3) don't "over improve" the property.

If you have trouble with the self-discipline required to save money, owning a house may help because you're forced to do it every month with a mortgage payment. At the end of the mortgage term, you'll own the place with a lot of equity in it, assuming you haven't done dumb things like spend your equity through second mortgages, home equity credit lines, and so on.

Once the mortgage is paid off, your costs for housing will plummet. In fact, those costs will likely be lower than renting. Have you been longing to dump your corporate job in favor of something you love but doesn't pay very well (like being an author, for example)? If so, then having a paid-off mortgage is a huge step toward making that financially feasible.

Finally, when you eventually sell the place, your beneficent Uncle Sam will currently let you exclude up to $250,000 in gains from taxation (if you are single) or $500,000 (if you are married filing jointly) when you file your taxes, assuming you have a gain on the sale. Not bad! Of course, by the time you sell, Uncle Sam might change the rules, so keep that in mind.

Buy Versus Rent

To help you evaluate the advantages and disadvantages of buying versus renting, take a look at the following tables. First, here are the pros and cons of buying a house or condo:

Pros and Cons of Buying

Pros	Cons
Possibility that the property will appreciate in value over time	Not liquid (hard to get money out)
Forced savings. Housing expense plummets when mortgage is paid off.	Unexpected expenses (things break or need to be replaced)
Possible capital gain tax exclusion upon sale	Depending on where you live, the after-tax cost might be a lot higher than renting
Don't have to deal with a landlord	Money sunk into house is not available for investment elsewhere
Emotional satisfaction of owning your own place	Expensive to maintain and sell
Uncle Sam may help defray some of the costs through the interest and property tax deduction	Might take a significant loss if forced to sell within a few years of purchase

Next, let's look at renting:

Pros and Cons of Renting

Pros	Cons
May be significantly less expensive than buying, depending on where you live	Money paid in rent is gone for good. Cost of moving is high.
Flexibility and low hassle	No possibility of building equity
Easy to move once lease is up	Landlord hassles
Expenses fixed and known for duration of lease	As rents rise with inflation over long periods of time, renting could become more expensive than owning
Landlord deals with maintenance	Potentially less emotional satisfaction
Money that might otherwise go to house down payment could be invested elsewhere	Limited or no control over property appearance and maintenance

If You Think You Might Buy...

If you are thinking about buying a house or condominium, consider the following:

- Before you start looking at properties, do the math. Know what you can afford and don't go above that amount.
- Loan: Avoid negative amortization. Avoid points unless you know for certain you'll be in the house a very long time and/or will not refinance. (And how could you know that in advance?) Avoid loans with pre-payment penalties. Get quotes from multiple lenders. Compare all the costs and fees before choosing one. Carefully read everything you sign. These are legally binding documents. Bring along an experienced, impartial person to help you review the documents
- Use an HP12C or equivalent financial calculator to try different scenarios and see how each would affect your payments. For example, vary the interest rate, the principal amount, 15 years versus 30, etc.

- Consider a 15-year mortgage. For me, a 15-year loan kept us from buying a house that was beyond our means and helped us pay off the mortgage quickly. With 30-year loans you're mostly paying interest the first several years and not reducing the principal very quickly. Here's where the financial calculator can be really helpful. For example, if you're borrowing $200,000:

Loan type	Interest Rate	Monthly Payment	Total Interest Payments
30-year fixed	5.5%	$1,136	$208,808
15-year fixed	5.0%	$1,582	$84,686
Difference		**$446**	**$124,122**

Notice that you're only paying $446 more per month in this example, but are saving $124,122 in interest expense to the bank. Granted, Uncle Sam may pay a portion when you take the mortgage interest tax deduction. However, you still end up paying most of it out of your own pocket.

You will own the house free and clear in 15 years rather than 30. I get a great deal of emotional satisfaction knowing that I am debt free. Do be aware, however, that you will have a lot of equity tied up in the house that could otherwise be invested or used for other purposes.

- Rather than a 15-year loan, you could consider taking out a 30-year mortgage. Then, make extra payments towards the principal as your income increases and/or as excess cash is available. You'd benefit from the lower monthly payment of a 30-year mortgage. Additionally, the optional extra payments would allow you to pay the loan off years earlier. You should consider this only if you are sure that you will not need the extra money that you're contributing to principal reduction. The only way to get the money back out is to sell the house or take out a home equity loan or a second mortgage. These loans generally come with higher interest rates than your first mortgage, so this would defeat the purpose of paying down the principal in the first place.
- Adjust your tax withholding at work once the purchase is completed. Since the mortgage interest expense and property tax are tax deductible, your tax burden may decline. (See the chapter on Uncle Sam.) Therefore, you likely won't need to have as much withheld from your regular paycheck.
- Your monthly cash flow requirements may be significantly higher than when you were renting. Estimate your new monthly cash needs, then make sure you still have a good emergency fund after your large down

payment. Now that you have the responsibility of owning a home, be sure you can still meet all your monthly cash needs for at least 3-6 months in the event you lose a job or have unexpected expenses.

- Plan for an annual maintenance/repair budget of 1% of the cost of the house. So on a $200,000 house, that's $2,000 a year or about $165 per month.
- Think of your house as a place to live, not an investment. Buy the place because you love it. Then, win or lose, you will not be disappointed. A good rule of thumb is that residential properties increase in value at slightly more than the rate of inflation over the very long term. If you get more than this, great! Just don't plan on it.
- Avoid the temptation to extract the equity from your home. You'll be bombarded with pitches from banks and mortgage brokers to take out second loans, home equity lines of credit (also called HELOCs), or so-called "cash-out" refinancing. If you do this, you'll be increasing your debt and further delaying the date when you own the place free and clear.

Some financial advisors recommend carrying as much debt as possible on the house so that your money can earn greater returns in the stock market or elsewhere. This might be good advice in a rising market. However, as we've seen over the past decade, good stock market returns cannot be taken for granted. In fact, you would have lost money in the stock market over the past decade. Rising house prices also cannot be taken for granted, as we saw in the last few years when housing prices declined nationally for the first time since the Great Depression of the 1930s.

I love our house and am glad that we're not at the mercy of a landlord. This is an emotional consideration that has nothing to do with the financial aspect of it, but it is a consideration nonetheless. I'm delighted that we own with no mortgage. Now that we're in our early 50s, it's a relief to have significantly lower monthly cash flow needs since the mortgage went away. We are actually paying far less to live in our house than the renter living down the street.

I hope this chapter has helped you evaluate some of the considerations that go into the rent vs. buy decision when you are evaluating a place to live. As we've seen, not all the considerations are financial. I suspect the Life Vision you developed earlier may also lend some insight that would help you think this through.

I'd encourage you to go back and review your Life Vision when you eventually confront what will likely be the biggest financial decision of your life. I'm confident you will make a choice that is in alignment with your life's goals and dreams!

SECTION IV

Investing

"*It is better to have a permanent income than be fascinating.*"
— OSCAR WILDE

CHAPTER 9

Investing Overview

"If a little money does not go out, great money will not come in."
— CONFUCIUS

Investing is by far the greatest part of the personal finance game. Start young, set aside regular amounts, invest prudently, and you'll get rich, slowly but surely. In the later years of your investing lifetime, your money could be growing faster in a typical year than you likely would make working at a job!

You won't want to play in this sandbox until you've built up a three to six month emergency cash fund that you could draw from in the event of job loss or other unexpected negative financial event. (Refer to Chapter 4, "*Getting Started*", for a refresher if necessary.) Investing is for long-term money that you won't need to access for several years or even until retirement.

Once you've built your emergency fund, you'll be patting your rapidly growing bags of cash and wondering, "Now what?" Or perhaps you have started a job with a company-sponsored retirement plan and you need to figure out where to direct your contributions.

This section of the book will help you understand how to make intelligent decisions as you wade into the world of investing. This chapter provides an overview of the most common investments. It also explains how mutual funds and Exchange Traded Funds (ETFs) work and why they are good options for novice investors. Chapter 10 covers bonds in detail. Chapter 11 does the same with stocks. Finally, in Chapter 12, I'll get you thinking about how to allocate your money across the investment universe.

I will reference several mutual funds from The Vanguard Group[10] (www.vanguard.com) in the next few chapters to use as examples. These funds represent low-cost generic "slices" of the stock and bond markets. Please do not interpret these examples as recommendations for you to purchase because they may or may not be appropriate for your situation. Other mutual fund companies offer low-cost, low-fee funds that may also serve you well. Consider using Morningstar.com® or Yahoo!® Finance to evaluate these or to search for others. You'll need to do your own research to determine what's best for you.

[10.] *Vanguard historical fund performance data, expense ratios, and fund portfolio information cited in the pages that follow are copyright © The Vanguard Group, Inc., used with permission.*

The pages that follow will help you figure out what to look for and how to assess what might be appropriate.

Don't Be Intimidated!

If you have no knowledge about investing, I want to reassure you right now that you do not need to feel intimidated. Many of the terms might be new, but the essence of investing is not very complicated. In these next chapters, I will introduce you to the concepts necessary to successfully invest in the most common types of assets. I will also help simplify the menu of choices that you'll have.

I know that it might be easier to simply go to a bank or credit union and deposit your spare cash into a Certificate of Deposit (CD) and be done with it. As you will see in a minute, that choice is unlikely to get you where you want to be financially. It is no harder to open an account with a brokerage firm or mutual fund company than it is to do so at a bank.

Allocating your money wisely and choosing among an array of investment products are probably the most difficult tasks an investor will face. By the time you are done with these next few chapters, you should be armed with the knowledge to make those choices. You can do this on your own or in consultation with a competent financial advisor. Either way, please do not avoid the choices simply because it looks scary at first! If an old goat like me can figure out how to use social media and the Internet to help market this book, then you can figure out how to invest wisely!

Prudent Risk-Taking

We've discussed several examples at various points in this book that show how easy it is to accumulate over $1,000,000 if you start early enough. You may remember in those examples that I usually assumed an 8% average return in the stock market over long periods of time. To do this, you will need to be comfortable with a certain amount of risk. (You might want to revisit Chapter 2, Principle #7, "Understand your risk tolerance," for a refresher.) It will be extremely difficult to accumulate huge bags of cash without venturing into the world of investing.

Here's a specific example to illustrate what I mean. In the first chapter, I mentioned that $4.25 per day invested at age 20 at an average annual return of 8% in the stock market would leave you with a balance of just over $1,000,000 at age 70. In contrast, a bank account earning 3% interest over the same period leaves you with only $177,139 fifty years later. That 5% difference in return means more than $800,000 fewer dollars in your pocket. If you wanted to end up with $1,000,000 but stick to a super-safe bank CD, you'd have to increase your contribution from about $125 per month to roughly $725!

Note that the above example ignores the taxes you'd need to pay along the way. Interest on bank CDs is payable annually at ordinary income tax rates, thereby reducing your ability to let the interest compound over long periods of time. In contrast, taxes on many stock market investments are currently subject to more favorable federal tax rates and are generally not levied until you sell the underlying security. (This being the tax code, there are of course exceptions. Stock mutual fund distributions are subject to tax along the way, for example. Consult your tax person with questions and for advice.)

Here's another reason to contemplate the possibility of taking on a bit of prudent risk. The good news is that it's not that hard to accumulate over $1,000,000 in your lifetime as long as you start early enough. The bad news is that, in 50 years, that amount of money will not buy nearly as much as it does today. This happens because of inflation, which is the tendency for prices to rise over time. (The opposite, where prices go down, is deflation, which happened during the 1930s in the USA and in the 1990s in Japan.) You've probably heard your parents and grandparents wax poetically about how a movie cost $0.25 or a gallon of gas was $0.40 in their day. You roll your eyes and think, "Oh man, here we go again." What's happened is inflation. And you will be making the same comments in 40 years to your grandkids, too.

Doubling Your Money

To demonstrate this, let me introduce you to the **Rule of 72**. This is a handy rule of thumb that you can use to approximate how long it will take a number to double. Let's use the Rule of 72 to show how damaging inflation can be. Let's assume that prices are expected to increase 3% per year. The Rule of 72 says to take 72 and divide it by the interest rate, as follows: 72/3%=24 years. So, your cost of living would approximately double every 24 years if the inflation rate is 3% per year. If you spend $2,000 per month now, this rule of thumb would tell you that the same set of things would cost $4,000 in 24 years. It would double again to $8,000/month in another 24 years when you are in your 60s and beyond. Ouch.

Don't get too depressed about this. Returning to the good news, your salary is likely to increase over time to help you keep up with inflation. You'll just need to make sure that your investments are staying ahead of inflation in the same way. That's why you'll need to consider deploying at least some percentage of your savings beyond the safe and dependable bank CD.

Using the Rule of 72 again, let's see how fast your money would double using an 8% average annual return in the stock market: 72/8%=9 years to double. In this scenario your investment money would be growing far faster over time than the expected rate of inflation. Remember, though, that the Rule of 72 is only an approximation and that the returns of your investment **portfolio**[11] will vary widely during your lifetime. However, this formula will at least give you a rule of thumb with which you can experiment. To get more precise numbers, you can use a financial calculator to run a variety of scenarios.

Types of Investments You Might Consider

In thinking about how to present this material to you, I decided to focus on stocks and bonds as the primary asset classes for your consideration. The benefits to this approach are: (1) stocks and bonds tend to be the most commonly available for the average investor; (2) they are generally very liquid (meaning they can be easily bought and sold); and (3) they are relatively easy to understand.

What Is a Bond?

A bond is debt issued by a corporation or a government entity. Think of it as an IOU. Bonds are issued in various amounts (called "**face value**"). They are sold to investors with a promise to pay interest at fixed intervals. Assuming the investor holds an individual bond to the end of its life (when it "**matures**") and the issuer does not go bankrupt in the interim, the face value, or principal, is returned to the investor. A bond may be worth more or less than its face value before it finally matures, depending on changes in market interest rates.

What Is a Stock?

When you own stock in a company, you are literally a part owner of that enterprise. Companies typically issue a large number of shares of stock (in the millions or billions, depending on company size), which are sold to investors. Individual investors (like you and me) and large institutions (like pension funds) purchase and sell shares on stock exchanges. The exchanges serve as marketplaces to match up those wanting to buy with those wanting to sell.

[11.] *Your portfolio is the set of investments that you own.*

Stock ownership allows you to participate in the success of companies large and small, domestic and international. Unlike a bond, which pays a fixed amount of interest, there is no artificial upper limit on the value of a share of stock. If a company continues doing well, then the share price should go up over time and the investors will be well rewarded. Of course, many companies are not successful and may fail completely. If that happens, the stockholders will lose money, possibly their entire investment.

Free enterprise is at the core of our capitalist system. Millions of entrepreneurs, managers, and workers are hard at work every day creating products and services that people want to buy. As the companies grow and prosper, all the stakeholders, including investors, will prosper as well. In my opinion, one of the best ways to participate and share in this success is through financial investments in the stock market. For me, it's also a great intellectual game and a lot of fun!

Alternatives to Stocks and Bonds

A well-diversified portfolio of stocks and bonds will serve most investors well. However, stocks and bonds are not the only game in town. You should be aware that there are other investment options available. When you read financial periodicals or books, you may come across alternative investments, some of which I will briefly describe below. Many of these alternatives require specialized knowledge and skill and may not be appropriate for a novice investor. For now, just be aware these choices exist. You may want to take a look at some of these options in several years after you have developed additional experience with investing. Here goes:

- **Rental real estate**: If you have a hankering to be a landlord and don't mind the occasional hassles associated with handling tenants, rental real estate can potentially offer decent long-term returns. Your wonderful Uncle Sam offers his help through various features of the tax code. These include the ability to depreciate the property to save on taxes and the possibility of deferring capital gains taxes by doing a "Section 1031 exchange" into a different property. The rules are complex, of course, so you will probably want to consult with an accountant if you want to pursue this route. One of the major downsides of owning rental real estate is that the money you invest is not very liquid. (That is, the asset is hard to dispose of and requires a lot of expense to do so.) If you are interested in learning more about rental real estate, please visit my website for a list of additional resources.

- **Real Estate Investment Trusts (REIT)**: If you like the idea of owning real estate but don't want the hassles, you could consider buying a publicly traded REIT through a stockbroker. REITs typically own dozens or hundreds of properties so the risk of a failure with any individual property is mitigated. REITs are required to distribute 90% of their income back to investors, so they typically pay fairly rich dividends. The other great advantage is that you can sell it inexpensively in five minutes through your broker if you decide you don't want to hold it anymore. Some REITs specialize in certain types of real estate, such as apartments or shopping centers. Others cover fairly broad portions of the real estate markets. Again, my website can refer you to other resources if you want to learn more.
- **Precious metals, commodities, stock options, currency trading, and other alternatives**: For those of you blessed (or cursed) with an overabundance of testosterone, you may come across these categories of investments and be tempted. I once bought a precious metals mutual fund because it was going up. That is a dumb reason to make an investment. I eventually sold it because I couldn't understand what drove the performance of the shares, other than investor excitement or disillusionment. Everything I've listed in this category is considered speculative and highly risky. I would stay away from these and let the professional investors play in this sandbox by themselves.

Mutual Funds

One way to assemble your portfolio is to do all the research on your own and pick individual stocks and bonds, one at a time. Frankly, this is difficult and probably not advisable for novice investors. Mutual funds are a better way to invest for those with little training or interest in this subject.

Mutual funds pool together money from a large number of investors. The money is then invested in stocks, bonds, short-term money-market instruments, or other securities. The benefits of a fund versus buying individual securities are many:

- You benefit from diversification. Mutual funds may own dozens or even hundreds of individual bonds or stocks. If one issuer goes bankrupt or loses value, the impact to you is likely negligible in the grand scheme of things.
- Someone else does the research to select individual stocks or bonds to purchase for the fund.
- They are easy to buy and sell and to reinvest your earnings back into them.

Types of Mutual Funds

There are a plethora of mutual funds available. Here are some of the most common types:

- **Stock funds (also called "equity funds"):** As the name implies, these mutual funds hold stocks, potentially hundreds, in a single fund. An amazing variety of investment styles is available, including funds that focus on growth stocks, value stocks, large company, small company, international, and so on. Depending on the underlying holdings, the fund may also pay out dividends to the investor.
- **Bond funds** hold a variety of debt securities issued by corporations or government entities. As with stock funds, bond funds hold large numbers of individual bonds, providing diversification and some protection in the event a small number of the holdings go bad. These funds generally pay out interest to the investor at regular intervals.
- **Money market funds** typically buy very high quality short-term debt or certificates of deposit from a variety of issuers and seek to maintain a constant net-asset-value (NAV) of $1 per share. They are among the safest mutual funds, but they are not guaranteed.
- **Balanced funds** hold a mix of stocks and bonds. They will typically strive to maintain a relatively constant ratio of each. A mix of 60% stocks and 40% bonds is typical, though it could vary somewhat. The fund's management discloses the chosen mix with the information they are required to provide potential investors.
- **Target Date funds (also called "lifecycle" funds):** These are "funds of funds" designed to simplify selection of mutual funds for those investing for retirement. The fund company automatically adjusts the holdings to become more conservative as the investor approaches retirement age.

Active Fund Management or Passive Indexing?

Since a mutual fund typically owns dozens or hundreds of individual securities, who selects what goes into the fund?

- An **actively managed** fund hires a bunch of smart and well-paid managers to select the individual stocks and/or bonds for inclusion in the fund. The goal, of course, is to choose securities that match the fund's investment objectives and that will (hopefully) outperform the market as a whole. As we will see later, this is not an easy thing to do. Actively managed funds tend to be burdened by higher costs, which are passed on to the investor. The higher expenses may mean a lower return to the investor unless the fund achieves its goal of beating the performance benchmark.

- **Index funds** seek to passively track an underlying benchmark or index. An index is a basket of dozens (or hundreds) of stocks or bonds that represent certain portions of the total market. The S&P 500® index is perhaps the best known. There are a plenitude of others. Index funds tend to have among the lowest fees because the management company doesn't need to spend as much money on research and paying salaries for high-priced fund managers.

Mutual Fund Fees

The downside of buying a mutual fund is that you have to pay fees to the fund company to compensate them for their expenses. Fair enough. However, remember that you are a guppy swimming with sharks. Many Wall Street firms have layered on a bunch of fees that can suck lots of money out of your pocket if you are not careful. Mutual fund fees may include some or all of the following:

- Management and administrative fees
- 12b-1 fee to cover marketing or distributing the fund
- Commission or "sales load" to pay the broker who sold you the fund. (Funds that do not apply this fee are called "no-load" mutual funds.)
- Purchase and redemption fees
- Account service fees

Here's the sneaky thing. You don't get a bill for some of these fees. Rather, they are subtracted from the fund's return so you never see it. You MUST read all the disclosures that come with the fund to see what the fee structure is. (Refer back to Chapter 2, Principle #5–*"Pay Attention."*) Let's take a look at what fees do to your investment performance over long time periods:

Fee Comparison: Contribute $125/Month @ 8.25% Average Annual Return (Before Fees) over 50 Years

	Balance After 50 Years
Fund with 0.25% fees	$991,466
Fund with 1.0% fees	$747,262
Impact of additional fees	-$244,204

From Ramen to Riches

A stock mutual fund with total fees of 0.25% will deliver a balance of $991,466 over 50 years, if you assume $125/month in contributions and an annual return of 8% after fees are applied.

Let's take the same fund with the same contributions from you and the same annual return, but apply 1% in annual fees, rather than 0.25%. The fund will deliver a balance of $747,262 over the same period. The extra 0.75% in fees ate up $244,204. Doesn't that make you mad?

Here's what I look for when trying to locate a low-cost mutual fund:

1. A fund that has no sales load (a no-load fund)
2. No 12b-1 fees
3. No commissions
4. Low (or zero) account service fees
5. An expense ratio of no more than 0.35% total fees applied on the fund. This is the total percentage of fund assets used for administrative, management, advertising (12b-1), and all other expenses.
6. I buy directly through the fund issuer rather than paying a broker commission.

There are many mutual funds in the marketplace that meet these criteria. Don't let a smooth talking salesperson convince you otherwise.

What's the Difference Between Mutual Funds and ETFs?

"ETF" refers to "Exchange Traded Fund," which is a relatively new entry in the investing derby. Though the legal structures are different, ETFs share many similarities with mutual funds. Both hold a variety of individual securities to help you diversify. They reduce the risk of a serious negative impact to your net worth if a single investment within the fund goes belly up or performs poorly. They are easy and inexpensive to buy and sell. However, they are distinct in a couple ways. Let's compare and contrast.

Mutual Funds

- Bought or sold at a price determined after the close of the stock markets.
- May often be purchased without a brokerage commission directly from the fund company. Therefore, they are useful for purchasing smaller amounts on a regular basis through an automatic investment plan.
- If the fund pays a dividend, it is very easy to reinvest that money back into the fund, if you so choose.
- May not be as tax efficient as an ETF. Many mutual funds report **capital gains distributions** to the investor, which is taxable income in the year paid. (Capital gains distributions result from profitable sales of securities

held by the fund.) So even if you don't sell any shares, you could have a tax bill that results from these distributions. This is not a concern if the fund is held in a tax-advantaged account like an IRA.

Exchange Traded Funds (ETF)

- Trade like a stock throughout the day on a stock exchange. You will know the precise purchase or sale price because the transaction will happen in real time.
- Are purchased and sold through a stock brokerage and a commission must usually be paid. (This is beginning to change. More firms are now offering commission-free ETFs.)
- The investor generally has better control of capital gains taxation with an ETF if held in a taxable account. Many ETFs have limited or no capital gains distributions along the way, unlike most actively managed mutual funds. However, please note that this is not always true. You will need to review the fund's literature for historical and expected distribution information. Also, if the ETF pays out a dividend, you will have to pay taxes on that just like you would with a stock dividend or mutual fund dividend. Again, the tax issue is not a concern when the ETF is held in a tax-advantaged account like an IRA.
- Since many ETFs are passively tracking an index, they will often have much lower fees than many mutual funds. (To be fair, many low-cost index funds are competitive in their fee structures with ETFs. You have to do your homework.)

Once you've determined that a particular stock or bond investment is appropriate for your portfolio, you should evaluate multiple mutual funds and ETFs that have similar investment objectives. It is just like comparison-shopping for yogurt at the grocery store. Find the product you like, read the label for the contents, and then purchase the one that meets your needs for the lowest cost. Simple! The pros and cons listed above should be of help in determining which is right for you.

Save Your Paperwork

One last thing before we dive into the details. Every time you buy or sell an investment, whether it's a stock, bond, mutual fund, or whatever, your brokerage or mutual fund management company will send you a confirmation. The confirmation will contain details of your purchase or sale. You must hang on to this paperwork for as long as you own the investment, which might be years.

Sales of investments are taxable events unless they are held in tax-advantaged accounts like IRAs. Once you finally sell, you will need the paperwork at tax time to figure out your capital gain or loss. You will need to report your profit or loss to Uncle Sam when you file your taxes, so the brokerage paperwork will be needed to correctly figure out your tax liability. If necessary, please review the relevant portions of Chapter 5 ("*Uncle Sam*") for a refresher on the difference between short-term and long-term capital gains from a tax perspective.

That completes our overview of the investing landscape. Now we're ready to begin a detailed review of stocks and bonds and how you might evaluate them for possible inclusion in your own portfolio. First up: bonds.

CHAPTER 10

Bonds: Where You Are the Lender

"Acquaintance. A person we know well enough to borrow from,
but not well enough to lend to."
— AMBROSE BIERCE

Ah, the banker's life. Lend out other people's money in the morning and spend the afternoon schmoozing at the country club. Wouldn't it be fun to switch roles? Now that you are accumulating those bags of extra cash, you can! You decide who you'd like to lend to, and then sit back and collect the checks.

In this chapter, I've grouped together a set of investment choices that focus on various types of debt, or interest-bearing securities. They have distinct differences and legal structures, but all are basically IOUs that are issued by corporations, governments, or other entities. An investor makes money through the interest or dividend payments made by the bond issuer or by the fund. An investor may also profit (or lose money) if the investment is sold, depending on the interest rate environment at the time of sale.

Though stocks often get more attention, bonds are an important part of a diversified portfolio. Bonds are not as boring as they might seem. During the first decade of this century, the S&P 500® stock index actually lost money. If you had instead put your cash into a long-term bond index fund, your money would have more than doubled!

Will a performance like that be repeated in the next 10 years? Who knows? If we move into a deflationary period, like the USA in the 1930s or Japan in the 1990s, bonds could continue to do well. If interest rates rise to more "normal" levels (or beyond), bonds will perform poorly.

Boring doesn't matter. Making money and spreading your risk (diversifying) does matter. You cannot predict in advance which asset class will perform well and which will stink. As we saw from the above example, sometimes when stocks perform poorly, bonds perform well. And vice versa. If you have a decent mix of both, you should end up with a respectable risk-adjusted performance. This will help you sleep well at night as your money grows.

The Short Story on Bonds and Money Market Funds

- Money market mutual funds typically own short-term high-quality debt.
- A bond is a debt security (an IOU) issued by a corporation or a government entity.
- Bonds generally make regular interest payments to the holder. At the end of the bond's life (maturity), the bond's face value is returned to the investor.
- The value of a bond may fluctuate during its life. As long as you hold the bond until maturity (and the issuer doesn't default), you will get your principal back.
- As market interest rates rise, the value of a bond will fall. When interest rates fall, the bond's value will rise.
- Bonds issued by various government entities (federal, state, and local) may offer certain tax benefits.
- Bond funds own dozens or hundreds of bonds. They therefore provide some diversification to spread risk.
- For many investors, bond funds are likely a better option than owning individual bonds.
- Stick to investment grade bonds. Leave "high yield" or "junk bonds" to the professionals.

Money Market Mutual Funds

Money market funds are a type of mutual fund that typically buys short-term high-quality debt from a variety of issuers. The holdings might include commercial paper (corporate IOUs), certificates of deposit, and short-term U.S. government obligations. The average maturity of the holdings in the fund tends to be 90 days or less.

Buying a money market mutual fund is like dipping your toe into the pool to test the water. It's very unlikely you'll get a shock to your system and even more unlikely that a shark will take a bite out of your big toe. Money market funds are among the safest investments, though they are not guaranteed. (During the financial panic of 2008, the government stepped in to temporarily guarantee assets in these funds. Don't depend on that guarantee still being there by the time you read this.)

These funds strive to keep a constant **Net Asset Value (NAV)** of $1 per share. That means each share costs a dollar when you buy it and you get the same price when you sell it. Your profit comes from the dividends paid out by the fund. The dividends will fluctuate up and down as short-term interest rates change. In their long history, there have only been a couple of occasions where one of these funds dropped below the $1 share price. In normal times, money market funds will offer a return somewhat higher than what you might see at a bank. Unlike a bank CD, you do not have to tie up your money for a pre-determined period of time. Many also offer a checking feature and automatic purchase/redemption from your bank account for easy access to your money.

I should note that as of this writing, the world financial system still has not returned to "normal." The **Federal Reserve** (a.k.a. "The Fed", the central bank of the United States) lowered interest rates to near zero during the financial panic of late 2008 and early 2009. The Fed's actions influence the movement of interest rates throughout the market. The dividends paid by money market mutual funds closely track the rates set by the Fed.

As of this writing, interest rates remain at that ultra-low level. Sadly, money market funds are now also paying near zero or have even closed to new investors. When interest rates gradually return to more normal levels, these funds might be worth a look as a place to park some of your short-term money or a portion of your emergency fund. (See the "*Getting Started*" chapter.)

The United States **Securities and Exchange Commission (SEC)** is responsible for regulating these and other mutual funds. The SEC website has more information on money market funds at **www.sec.gov/answers/mfmmkt.htm**.

Bonds

A bond is a debt security (an IOU) issued by a corporation or a government entity. The issuer typically uses the funds to finance their operations or to make investments in property or equipment. The issuer is obligated to make interest payments at prescribed intervals until the bond matures, at which point the original amount borrowed is repaid to the bondholder.

Here are some of the important terms you'll need to understand when thinking about bonds:

- **Principal or "face value"**: Refers to the amount of money upon which the issuer will pay interest.

- **Maturity**: The date at which the bond "matures" and the face value of the bond is repaid to the bondholder. Maturities can range from under a year to more than 30 years.
- **Interest rate**: Expressed as a percentage of the bond's face value, this rate determines how much will be paid to the bondholder at pre-defined intervals. (You may also hear the term "coupon", which is the amount of interest paid to the investor.)
- **"Callable"**: Bonds with this feature allow the issuer to repay the bond early, generally no sooner than some specified date. Callable bonds may be disadvantageous to the buyer because the issuer generally will only repay early if interest rates have dropped significantly. If interest rates rise in the open market, then the issuer would rather continue paying you the lower rate on the bond they originally issued.

Types of Bonds

Some bonds are considered **investment grade**, because they are of higher quality with lower risk of **default** (the issuer going bankrupt or reneging on their obligations). At the other end of the spectrum are **"high yield"** or speculative issues. These are sometimes called **"junk bonds"** because the credit-worthiness of the issuer is not as sound. Just like individuals have credit ratings, so do bond issuers. Credit rating firms like Fitch, Moody's, and Standard and Poor's rate credit quality of corporations, like Equifax and Experian rate credit risk for individuals.

You can find bonds issued by corporations where the interest is fully taxable. Or perhaps you'd like to buy Treasury bonds, notes, or bills issued by the U.S. Treasury which are federally taxable, but exempt from state income tax. How about **municipal bonds,** which are issued by states or local governments and may be fully tax-exempt? Sigh. You have a growing pile of cash to invest and so little time to digest all this.

Can You Lose Money?

But wait, there's more. Can you lose money on a bond? Absolutely! The easiest way is to buy a junk bond from an issuer in financial difficulty. If the issuer declares bankruptcy, you stand in line with all the other creditors to pick through the carcass of the deceased entity. The good news with corporate bonds is that bondholders are higher in the pecking order than those holding the company's stock in the event of bankruptcy. If you're lucky, you might get some fraction of the amount owed.

Another way to potentially lose money is to sell the bond before it has matured. This could happen if current market interest rates for a bond of the same duration are higher than the interest rate that your bond is paying. There are many moving parts in bond mathematics, but let me give you an overly simplified example:

- Let's say you buy a newly issued one-year bond for $1,000. It pays 5% interest at maturity. Therefore, the total value of your investment when the bond matures is the $1,000 principal plus $50 interest or $1,050 total.
- Assume that the day after you bought the bond, interest rates rise unexpectedly and similar bonds are now paying 6% interest. The value of this newer bond is $1,060 ($1,000 principal plus $60 interest)[12].
- Now you want to sell your bond. If you were a buyer, would you want to purchase your bond worth $1,050 or the newer bond worth $1,060? The only way you'd be able to sell your bond is to sell at a discount from the original value of $1,000 (let's say $990). A buyer paying $990 for your bond would get back $1,000 from the issuer at maturity plus the $50 interest, leaving a profit of $60. This makes the value of the two bonds equivalent. Thus, you took a $10 loss on your investment. Make sense?

Conversely, of course, you could potentially sell your bond for a profit through your broker if market interest rates have declined. In this situation your bond is paying an above-market interest rate so it is worth more. This is why people say "bond prices move inversely to interest rates." In other words, when interest rates go up, bond prices go down. And vice versa.

The market value of a bond may fluctuate during its lifetime. It could be worth more or less than its face value if it is sold before it matures. If you hang on until maturity, the issuer will pay the face value.

Once Again, Uncle Sam Is Your Friend

In my many years of investing, the only individual bonds I have purchased have been from my Uncle Sam. I'm confident he's going to pay me back and therefore do not need to do any research to determine whether his bonds are safe. The federal government issues a huge variety of debt securities. The issues include:

[12.] *In reality, it is extremely unlikely that interest rates would move this quickly. I wanted to keep this simple to illustrate the concept.*

- **Treasury Bills (T-bills):** These have maturities ranging from a few days to one year.
- **Treasury Notes:** Are issued in maturities of 2, 3, 5, 7, and 10 years. Interest is paid semi-annually.
- **Treasury Bonds:** Mature in 30 years and pay interest twice a year.
- **Treasury Inflation Protected Securities (TIPS):** These are issued with 5, 10, and 30-year maturities. TIPS are unusual in that the principal is adjusted by changes in the Consumer Price Index (CPI). The principal increases with inflation and decreases with deflation. When the bond matures, the investor is paid the adjusted principal or the original principal (whichever is greater). TIPS pay interest every six months. The great benefit with these securities is that you have some measure of inflation protection that most other bonds do not have. The serious downside is that if you hold these in a taxable account, income tax is due annually on both the cash interest payments and the principal adjustment. The bummer is that the principal adjustment is not actually paid to you until the bond matures or until you sell the bond. Therefore, many advisors recommend that you only hold these securities in a tax-advantaged account like an IRA. That way you don't have the annual hassle of dealing with the tax consequences.
- **U.S. Savings Bonds (Series I):** If you want some inflation protection in a taxable account without the hassles of TIPS, Series I Savings Bonds might be a good choice. Federal taxes are deferred until you actually redeem the bond. We discussed these in some detail back in Chapter 5 ("*Uncle Sam*"), so you can refer back to that section for a refresher if you'd like.
- **U.S. Savings Bonds (Series EE):** Again, please refer to Chapter 5 for details describing the features of Series EE Savings Bonds. They are another super-safe and easy choice for individual investors.

Remember that the debt securities issued by Uncle Sam are exempt from state and local income taxes. Your after-tax yield will likely be somewhat higher than a fully taxable corporate bond paying the same interest rate, depending on state and local taxes. U.S. Government bonds can be purchased from the U.S. Treasury at **www.treasurydirect.gov.**

Bond Mutual Funds

Other than debt issued by the federal government, everything else that's for sale in the bond market requires a lot of work to determine the credit quality, whether the bond is callable, the appropriate mix of maturities, and so on. For my bond investments, I generally buy a bond mutual fund or a bond Exchange Traded Fund (ETF). As we saw in earlier chapters, the benefits of a fund versus buying individual bonds are many:

- You benefit from diversification. Bond funds may own dozens or even hundreds of individual bonds. If one issuer goes bankrupt, the impact to you is likely negligible in the grand scheme of things.
- Someone else does the research for you, based on some objective criteria. The fund managers have a lot more training and expertise than you and I could ever hope to acquire on our own.
- It's easy to sell a fund whenever you want or to reinvest your earnings back into the fund.

So Which Bond Fund(s) Should I Buy?

The number of choices can be overwhelming. Using Vanguard® as an example, I currently find 27 bond funds listed on their website. Again, I won't be giving you investment advice, but one way to narrow the list would be to focus on the index funds. Bond index funds simply try to passively track the performance of a particular benchmark that reflects a subset of the overall bond market.

If an index fund properly matches its holdings to the target benchmark, your results should closely track the average performance of the fund's market segment. Index funds generally have very low expense ratios as well. Since it is pretty difficult for even professional managers to "beat the market," index funds should serve most investors well. Vanguard has four of these:

- Short-Term Bond Index: average maturity of 1-5 years
- Intermediate-Term Bond Index: average maturity of 5-10 years
- Long-Term Bond Index: average maturity of 15-30 years
- Total Bond Market Index: average maturity of 6.6 years

The selection now becomes much simpler. Here are some general things to consider when you're looking at a bond fund:

- **Interest rate environment**: When interest rates are falling, bond funds tend to rise in value for the same reason we discussed earlier with the individual bonds. That is, the individual bonds held in the fund are likely paying higher interest rates than the new market rates, thereby making them more valuable. Conversely, when interest rates are rising, bond funds tend to decline in value.
- **Duration**: In normal times, short-term bond funds tend to pay lower rates of interest than long-term funds. Typically investors will demand higher interest rates to loan out their money for very long periods because they

are concerned about inflation risk and other factors. Occasionally the reverse happens and short-term bonds pay out more than longer-term bonds. (This is called an **"inverted yield curve."**) When this happens, the bond market might be signaling that an economic slowdown is coming or a belief that inflation will remain low over the long term.

- **Volatility:** The share prices of long-term funds tend to be more volatile because they are more sensitive to fluctuations in interest rates.
- **Investment grade only:** I only consider funds holding investment grade bonds. I won't touch anything with speculative or junk bonds in the portfolio. A market professional might be able to figure out how to make money on junk bonds. I personally would rather not take the risk.
- **Municipal bond funds:** These might be worth a look if your income is fairly high. These funds hold bonds that are issued by state and local governments or other public entities. The interest rate you can earn is generally lower than other types of bonds. However, the advantage is that the interest payments are often (but not always) exempt from both federal and state income taxes, which make them potentially attractive to individuals in high tax brackets.
  - ○ Given the precarious financial situation in which many states and municipalities currently find themselves, beware of **credit risk**. It is not unheard of for issuers to default, though so far defaults in municipal markets are relatively uncommon. The good news with owning a fund is that the credit risk from a single issuer is mitigated. However, the bad news is that "double tax exempt" funds typically concentrate their holdings in one specific state to qualify for both the federal and state tax exemptions. That concentration can increase risk. For example, the financial health of cities in California tends to be more correlated with each other than with cities in other states.
  - ○ If you're fortunate enough to have an income that is high enough to give some consideration to municipal bonds (a high class problem), then you could also afford to consult with your tax advisor to determine whether these might make sense for you.

That's it for the introductory tutorial on money market funds, bonds, and bond funds. We've covered what they are and how they work. We have not yet discussed how they might figure in the overall mix of your investments. Later on, we'll talk about how you might think about allocating your money across bonds, stocks, and other potential investments. In the next chapter, we'll continue on to my favorite investment class of all: stocks.

CHAPTER 11

Stocks Rock! (And Sometimes Shock)

"October. This is one of the peculiarly dangerous months to speculate in stocks. The others are July, January, September, April, November, May, March, June, December, August, and February."

— MARK TWAIN

I had my introduction to the stock market in the early 1990s. The country was in recession and the auto industry was going through its once-a-decade meltdown. My attention turned to Chrysler, which had gone through near-death experiences many times during industry downturns. I bought the stock after it had fallen from $30 to around $15. Since the stock was paying a nice fat dividend of 7%, I figured all I had to do was sit around and collect the dividend check until the company and industry recovered. Well, shortly after I bought the stock, the company eliminated the dividend and the stock fell to $7. Suddenly I wasn't looking too smart. The one thing I had in my favor was patience, which was rewarded a few years later. I ended up tripling my money. I was hooked! (A quick coda to the Chrysler story: during the downturn of the late 2000s, Chrysler did indeed finally declare bankruptcy and its private equity shareholders were wiped out.)

The great thing about the stock market is that you literally become a part owner of the company in which you buy **shares**, which represent fractional ownership or **equity** in the firm. You don't need to be a billionaire to own a piece of some of the greatest enterprises this country has produced. Granted, the billionaire can often buy the entire company and we mortals only get to buy a piece, but who's to quibble? Some of the most successful corporations can go on growing for decades, making their shareholders fabulously wealthy. Can you imagine if you had been an early buyer of Apple? Wal-Mart? How about Coca Cola? The list goes on and on.

The Short Story on Stocks

- You become a part owner of the company in which you buy **shares**, which represent **equity** in the firm.
- Some stocks pay **dividends** to the investor, which represent a portion of the company's profits that they choose to return to its shareholders.
- A profitable sale of a stock or mutual fund is called a **capital gain**. (The opposite is called a **capital loss**.)
- Stocks are not risk-free investments. You assume the risk of principal loss and **volatility**.
- The stock market sometimes delivers years of poor performance (during the first decade of the 2000s, for example). Conversely, sometimes years of above-average returns are seen (such as during the 1990s).
- For most novice investors, mutual funds or ETFs are better choices than buying individual stocks.
- You should not buy individual stocks unless you are willing to invest the time to do research, are comfortable making mistakes, and have enough cash to **diversify**.
- Actively managed funds tend to be burdened by higher expenses. They may have to outperform the market by a significant amount before they will beat an index fund.
- You need to learn about the many types of investing choices available (growth, value, international, etc.) to see what fits your needs and risk tolerance.

A significant limitation of bonds is that when the bond matures, you will get back the face value plus any interest owed and no more. That limitation does not apply when buying shares of a company. As long as the company continues to grow and prosper, over the long run the stock should continue rising with no artificial upper bound. Isn't that awesome? That is one of the great attractions of the stock market. You can financially participate in the success and growth of companies large and small. The financial rewards can sometimes be astounding.

In addition, some stocks also pay regular or periodic **dividends** to the investor, which represent a portion of the company's profits that they choose to return to its shareholders. In situations like this, you have the possibility of both a **capital gain** in the value of the share price and a wonderful bonus of some cash that flows back into your pocket.

Of course, for every great success story, there are piles of losers that petered out and left their shareholders in tears. Think General Motors for a moment. One of America's greatest and largest companies for years, if not decades, it finally succumbed and filed for bankruptcy in 2009. To a shareholder of the 1960s that would have been unthinkable.

So, the moral of the story is that the stock market offers potentially limitless rewards but also significant risk of losing money. Perhaps all your money if you invest unwisely.

You'll sometimes hear of the **risk/reward tradeoff** or **risk premium**. That is, to earn a greater financial return, you'll need to be comfortable with a greater risk of loss. When the risk of loss is higher, investors demand a higher return to compensate them for the risk.

With stocks, you are definitely moving much further along the risk/reward scale than you would with money market funds, for example. That is why the long-term average return of the stock market is several percentage points higher than a bank CD or money market fund. The downside is that you assume the risk of loss of principal and **volatility** (the value of your shares going up and down, rather than remaining constant).

Historical Stock Market Performance

Any cash you commit to the stock market should be money that you are fairly certain you will not need for several years. The stock market can deliver poor performance for long periods of time. You would not want to be forced to sell during a market downturn. On the flipside, the market can also deliver significantly above-average performance for extended periods.

Let's take a look at some historical performance examples of the **Dow Jones Industrial Average (DJIA).** This index captures the performance of 30 large industrial companies. The index members change from time to time. It currently includes such stalwarts as IBM, Wal-Mart, Coca Cola, and Kraft Foods. It is one of the oldest and most famous of the stock market averages.

First, here are three periods where the DJIA went nowhere[13]:

Duration	Start/End Dates	DJIA Start	DJIA End
24 years	1/1929-1/1953	307	281
12 years	1/1963-1/1975	647	632
9 years	1/2001-1/2010	10,646	10,618

In the above examples, the Dow 30 average started and ended at nearly the same position over periods ranging from 9 years to 24 years. That is a very long time to wait! Of course, the numbers bounced all over the place during those periods, but bottom line is they went nowhere.

Now let's look at three **bull markets**, where prices were generally rising during the time periods in question:

Duration	Start/End Dates	DJIA Start	DJIA End	Percent Gain
19 years	1/1981-1/2000	875	11,723	1,240%
23 years	1/1942-1/1965	113	969	758%
9 years	1/1991-1/2000	2,611	11,723	349%

Wow, now we're talking some serious profits! During the first two periods shown in the table above, the DJIA multiplied more than 13 and 8 times, respectively. In the 1990s, the Dow 30 multiplied 4.5 times in only nine years.

Stock Market Volatility

As you've likely seen in the news media, the volatility of the stock market can be like a stomach-churning roller coaster. The market can move in erratic swings, either up or down, during relatively short periods. For example, the DJIA went from 10,850 in September 2008 to below 7,000 in March 2009 then back up to 10,700 in March 2010. From peak to trough, that represented a loss of about 40% during those 18 months. On the upswing from March 2009 to March 2010, investors saw a 60% gain. Now that's volatility! If you had been hibernating those 18 months and checked the Dow at the beginning of your nap and again when you woke up, it would look like nothing had happened the entire time.

[13.] *The DJIA examples ignore any dividends paid during the listed periods. At certain times in history, dividends made up a significant portion of the market's total return. The last few decades, dividends have been a smaller part of an investor's total return from the overall market.*

If you decide to allocate some of your hard-earned money to the stock market, you'll need to think about how you would react during such periods, particularly on the downside. Would you panic and sell? Or would you hold on knowing that eventually your patience would be rewarded? How would (or did) you feel if you were one of the unlucky investors who bailed out at the bottom in March 2009? It's important that you consider these questions if you are to be a stock market investor. (Refer back to Principle #7, "*Understand Your Risk Tolerance*", in Chapter 2.)

Should You Buy Individual Stocks?

I will pose the same question that I did earlier in the chapter on bonds: "Is it a good idea for a novice investor to buy an individual stock?" I am a huge fan of the stock market and I love buying individual stocks for my own accounts. At the same time, I have made many expensive mistakes. It's a wonderful intellectual game that requires a willingness to learn, patience, practice, and a commitment of time. In the end, it does not require that you be a rocket scientist. However, you really need to have a passion for it, a tolerance for volatility and loss, and a willingness to make a strong commitment to have a good chance at being successful.

For those reasons, I believe that novice investors should consider stock mutual funds or Exchange Traded Funds (ETFs) for their equity investments rather than buying individual stocks.

If You Decide to Try Stock Picking on Your Own

That said, if you are passionate about becoming a stock picker and have the time and inclination to do the research and pay attention, you might consider allocating a small portion of your investable assets to building your own stock portfolio. By small portion, I mean no more than 10-20% at the beginning. Until you can prove to yourself that the performance of your stock selections is greater than or equal to the overall market over a reasonable period of time, the rest of your long-term money would likely be better invested in stock and bond mutual funds or ETFs.

I also would strongly suggest you not buy individual stocks until you can answer, "yes," to each of the following questions:

1. Do you have enough money to buy at least 10-15 stocks across a variety of industries to mitigate the negative impact that may result from one or more of the companies suffering poor results?
2. Are you willing to take a complete loss on the money? This is not likely if you own quality companies in several industries. It is possible, however,

to lose most or all of it if you make poor selections. (Think WorldCom, Enron, General Motors, etc.)

3. Have you done your homework and learned how to evaluate a stock's prospects?

4. Have you tried your luck constructing a model portfolio built with play money? There are many websites available that will let you assemble a portfolio of stocks you'd like to track without actually buying them. You can then watch for free to see how your selections perform.

5. Are you willing to monitor your stock portfolio on a regular basis to prune the losers and allow the winners to grow?

If you want to build your own stock portfolio, you will need at least 10-15 individual stocks in companies that are in broadly different industries. This is called **diversification**. For example, if you know the airline industry well and buy 12 stocks in that industry, you are not diversified because stocks in the same industry are often **correlated** with each other. That is, if one stock in that industry goes up, the others have a tendency to do the same to some degree or other—and vice versa during industry downturns. Continuing with the airline industry as an example, let's say that the price of oil skyrockets as it did a few years ago. Given that fuel is a huge component of an airline's cost structure, guess what happens to airline stocks when the price of gas goes up dramatically? That's right, they all get clobbered.

I have paid a great deal of "tuition money" on individual stock purchases. I have more than my fair share of stupid investments that in hindsight I should not have made. I always learned a lot. Sometimes it cost me more than it should have. I'd caution you to approach this carefully. You should certainly build a "model portfolio" with play money first so that you can see how your investing instincts are working out.

Do not underestimate the time it will take to gain competence in stock selection. Market professionals take years learning this stuff. It's not necessarily complicated. However, the time investment is necessary if you want to have decent prospects for success. If you buy stocks without performing competent research, you are just gambling.

Similarly, once you make a purchase decision, you cannot just ignore it. You will need to regularly monitor the performance of all your holdings to see if the reasons you made the purchase continue to be true. Analyzing and selecting stocks is a topic that has been well trodden by other authors who are more competent and knowledgeable than I am. That is why you will not find a detailed dissertation on that here. If you're interested in learning more, I have included suggested resources on my website.

If You Decide You'd Rather Buy a Fund

For many investors, a mutual fund is an easy and inexpensive way to buy a basket of stocks. The benefits of a stock mutual fund are similar to the benefits we discussed earlier with bond mutual funds. Specifically:

- Stock mutual funds will own dozens or hundreds of individual stocks, giving you great diversification. If a few of the stocks in the fund perform poorly, the overall impact to the investor should be insignificant. (Of course, if the entire market experiences a meltdown, then the mutual fund will too.)
- Someone else does the research and stock selection for you.
- It's easy to sell a fund or to reinvest your earnings back into the fund.

Actively Managed Fund or Index Fund?

If you decide to buy a mutual fund, it is important to understand the distinction between an actively managed fund and an index fund. Actively managed funds have a bunch of well-paid managers applying their knowledge to select stocks for the fund that they feel will provide a good return. The hope, of course, is that the set of stocks they purchase will outperform the market as a whole. We will see shortly that this is not an easy thing to do.

An index fund, on the other hand, buys and holds a set of stocks that comprise a benchmark index of some subset of the overall market. (In fact, there are now indexes that look to reflect the entire market as a whole.) Perhaps the best known is the **S&P 500®** **index**. It is made up of 500 of the largest and most actively traded stocks. The S&P 500® is often regarded as a good proxy for the performance of the overall stock market. So, if you own an index fund that tracks the S&P 500®, you are effectively purchasing the average performance of the market as a whole. Index funds, then, are passive funds because they just buy shares of companies in the particular index that they are tracking.

The fund companies that offer an index fund like this don't have to do any research. They simply buy shares of each company proportionally to its representation in the index. Since there is no research to perform, these funds tend to have very low fees. The Vanguard S&P 500 index fund, for example, has an expense ratio of only 0.18%. The smaller the expense ratio, the greater proportion of the fund's return that goes back to you, the investor.

So maybe you're thinking, "Well, why would I only want to get the average performance of the stock market? I've always been better than average at everything I do. I always buy the best products and will not ever settle for average."

Well, in my years as a stock market observer and avid consumer of investment literature, I have to tell you that average actually ends up being above average most of the time. Let me explain.

If you buy an actively managed stock fund, you are paying a fund company for the expertise of their fund managers to pick stocks for you. Their goal, of course, is to "beat the market." With so many bright managers, backed up with all the wonders that computers and modern portfolio science bring, you would think that these guys would be able to reliably and significantly outperform a simple passive market index like the S&P 500®, right?

Nope. It turns out the vast majority of actively managed funds underperform their passive brethren, particularly as you stretch out the time horizon over long periods.

Occasionally the media will anoint some fund manager the stock-picking guru of the year or decade or whatever. That sort of media attention brings fame to the manager and plenty of new money for the fund. One such manager outperformed the market from 1991 to 2005–quite a feat! Unfortunately, fate intervened during the stock market meltdown of 2008-2009. The fund's manager made some big bets that turned out to be disastrous. The fund's 10-year performance ranking went from the top to near the bottom in fairly short order. Vaunted guru no more.

Poor stock selection is one reason why actively managed funds may underperform. Another significant explanation is that they are often handicapped by their expense structures and by the fees they charge. Let's do a quick refresher on the negative impact that fees have on your profits. Some of the fees you might see are:

- Management and administrative fees;
- **12b-1** fee to offset costs of marketing and distribution; and
- Commission or **sales load** to pay to the broker who sold you the fund.

If an S&P 500® index fund returns 8% after subtracting a 0.18% expense ratio, an actively managed fund with a 1% expense ratio would need a return of 9% just to break even with the index. Here's the thing: the fund collects their fees whether or not they outperform their benchmark. Remember that.

The difference of 0.82% in fees may not sound like much. However, it really adds up over the long term. We've talked about this before, but it bears repeating. Assume $125 per month in contributions over 50 years and an annual return of 8.18% before expenses and fees are applied. The low fee fund with the 0.18% expense ratio will leave you with over $250,000 more in your pocket at the end when compared with the fund charging 1%.

I do not want to leave you with the impression that I have never owned an actively managed fund, because I have. In particular, I've owned some special purpose funds in the past that targeted certain areas of the market where I had no expertise, but where I thought good gains were to be had. I also still own a balanced fund in my retirement account. (A balanced fund holds a mix of stocks and bonds.) That fund has served me well over the years and has a tolerable 0.35% expense ratio.

If you decide to buy an actively managed fund, you should be looking to buy a fund with: (1) no sales load; and (2) a low expense ratio, preferably less than 0.35%. You should have a good reason why you are choosing that fund over an index. The fund manager's picture on a magazine cover as "Fund Manager of the Decade" is not a good reason, as we saw in the earlier example. Remember, "Past performance is not a guarantee of future results." Amen.

Mutual Fund or ETF?

Don't forget that you will generally have a choice of a traditional stock mutual fund or an Exchange Traded Fund (ETF) when you want to make an investment in a basket of stocks. We covered this back in Chapter 9 (*"Investing Overview"*), so I won't repeat it here. I'd encourage you to review that section to refresh your memory on the advantages and disadvantages of each.

What About International Stocks?

Do not ignore international investments, as significant growth occurs in economies outside the United States. With international stocks, you are increasing your diversification and positioning yourself to take advantage of growth overseas.

With foreign stocks, be aware that one more variable is being introduced into the mix. Changes in the value of the foreign currency against the U.S. dollar can influence your results, either positively or negatively. When the foreign currency strengthens against the dollar, your returns improve. The opposite happens when the foreign currency weakens[14]. The Securities and Exchange Commission (SEC) has a good brochure on this topic at **www.sec.gov/investor/pubs/ininvest.htm**.

Investment Styles of Stock Mutual Funds or ETFs

As we saw in the last chapter, there are many bond indexes. The same is true for stocks. Each index targets a specific part of the stock-investing

---

[14.] *Some funds that hold foreign stocks attempt to mitigate this risk with currency hedging strategies. This is a complex subject that we won't cover here.*

universe. A couple even attempt to cover it all. Here is a sampling of the more common indexes that have corresponding mutual funds and ETFs that track them:

Domestic Stocks

- **S&P 500® Index**: We've already covered this one. It's a good proxy for the performance of larger U.S. companies.
- **Large-cap Index**: "Cap" refers to "capitalization", which is simply the price of a company's stock times the number of shares outstanding. It is a measure of the market value of the company. "Large cap" stocks are the big guys. Think Apple, Exxon, AT&T and the like.
- **Mid-cap Index**: A set of mid-sized corporations.
- **Small-cap Index**: The small fry. You probably have never heard of most of these companies.
- **Social Responsibility Index**: A set of companies that have been screened to meet certain social and environmental criteria.
- **REIT Index**: Publicly traded Real Estate Investment Trust companies, which focus on (you guessed it) real estate.

International Stocks

- **Emerging Markets Index**: An index of international developing markets, such as Brazil, Russia, India, and China.
- **European Index**: Pretty self-explanatory.
- **Pacific Index**: An index of stock markets in the Asia-Pacific region.
- **Total International**: Provides exposure to global (non-U.S.) stock markets.
- **Total World**: Invests broadly across the world's markets, including the U.S.

Have I managed to completely overwhelm you? I hope not. Even if I have, don't worry. In the next chapter, we'll cover how to simplify the choices that you face on where to put your money and how to allocate it across the major investment classes.

CHAPTER 12

Where Do You Stash Your Bags of Cash?

"Patience and perseverance have a magical effect before which difficulties
disappear and obstacles vanish."
— JOHN QUINCY ADAMS

When you have mastered the financial basics, have an emergency fund established, are diligently saving every month, and are ready to invest money for the long term, you should first stop and congratulate yourself! You are well on your way to having a wonderful financial life where money is serving you and not vice versa.

Hopefully, you are looking at those lovely bags of cash growing larger by the day. Your challenge now is to figure out how to put that money to work. In this chapter, we will discuss some of the choices you face as you decide how to allocate the money you have earmarked for long-term investments. The tough part is that you will ultimately need to make these decisions for yourself. A financial professional can help with recommendations if you choose that route. In the end, however, the choice will be yours.

Every person's situation is different. Some of you, for example, may have a very high risk tolerance; others very low. Each of you may be in a different stage of life—some single, some married, some with kids (or planning on having them). Some of you will have extravagant lifestyle choices with high cash needs. Others have very simple requirements. There is no one-size-fits-all answer.

You may ultimately choose to pay a professional to guide you. That is absolutely fine. You should not be embarrassed if you feel more comfortable with that approach. At a minimum, this chapter should help you understand what your investment professional is talking about and how to ask questions that will serve your best interests. For those of you comfortable managing investments on your own, I hope the educational material that follows will provide you with helpful information about thinking through your decisions.

Investing Is for Long-Term Money

Before we start, let's make sure we're clear on something. In the pages that follow, you will learn how to invest money that you will not need for several years or even decades. If you will need the money in the next few years, you are better off putting it in a guaranteed savings account rather than in more risky investments like the stock market.

As we saw earlier, investments can be volatile and can deliver lousy results for sometimes lengthy time periods. (Remember that investors in the S&P 500® stock index actually lost money for the entire decade of the 2000s. Even a five or ten year period may not be long enough.) The longer your time horizon, the more likely you will get the results you want.

To get you thinking for the really long term, I will orient the discussion around money that you want to invest for retirement. Some of you may have just started a job and want to start participating in your company's 401(k) plan. Others may already have an emergency fund in place and want to open an IRA with some of their extra cash. Great! This chapter will help you think about those decisions.

Even though the conversation will sound like retirement, the concepts and principles that we will review here apply for any long-term investment. So, if you think you might need the money for something big in 10 years and want to invest it in something with greater growth potential than a savings account, the remainder of this chapter will equip you to do that.

Investment Classes and Level of Risk

How do you balance your risk tolerance against the desire to make the cash pile grow as large as possible? You will need to figure out how to generate enough growth in your portfolio to live comfortably in your later years and support the other life goals you may have. We will talk more in the next chapter about how big your "magic number" may need to be to achieve these goals. The answer depends on a number of variables, including your current age, risk tolerance, when you want to retire, expected rate of return on your investments, and so on.

Let's first review the common classes of investments, ranked approximately from lowest risk (lower return) to higher risk (potentially higher return):
- Insured bank Certificate of Deposit (CD) or Treasury bill
- Money market mutual funds
- Short-term bond funds
- Intermediate-term bond funds
- Inflation-protected bond funds
- Long-term bond funds
- Domestic stock funds
- Real Estate Investment Trusts (REITs)

- International (developed countries) stock funds
- Emerging economies stock funds
- Other riskier alternative investments (not recommended unless you have significant amounts of money that you can risk)

If you invest all your money in bank CDs, money market funds, and short-term bond funds, you will likely sleep well. It's also unlikely you will end up with enough money at the end to support yourself in retirement, unless you are an extremely aggressive saver.

Investments concentrated entirely in the riskier areas will likely deliver pretty good growth over the very long term. You are also guaranteed an occasional wild ride that might cause gastrointestinal distress.

Appropriately spreading your money across all (or most) of these investment classes should give you a favorable risk-adjusted return. Using history as a guide, the riskier assets should deliver the best growth and the more conservative will take some of the bumps out of the ride. Of course, nothing is guaranteed or certain. Historical returns are a good benchmark, but returns in the future may not always behave as they have in the past.

Asset Allocation

Your challenge will be figuring out how to spread your money around in these different areas. In the investing world, this is called **asset allocation**. By investing in a variety of investment classes (stocks, bonds, real estate, and so on), you achieve broad diversification in your holdings. By diversifying, you reduce the level of risk and volatility in your portfolio. This improves the probability of getting the return you want and matching it with a level of risk that makes you comfortable. As always, however, there are no guarantees. (The exception is an FDIC-insured bank CD. We've already covered the pros and cons of that option.)

Let's look at some actual data so that you may see why diversifying across a variety of asset classes can help you. Here are the average annual returns of a selection of Vanguard's market index funds from 3/31/2000 through 3/31/2010:

Index Fund	10-Year Average Annual Return
S&P 500® index	-0.73%
Total bond market index	+5.98%
Total stock market index	-0.07%
Long-term bond index	+7.26%
REIT (real estate) index	+11.18%

If I had been clairvoyant, I would have put all my money in REIT and long-term bond funds the last 10 years because they significantly outperformed everything else. Stock market investors actually lost money during that period (admittedly not a great decade for investing in equities). Investors who were well diversified with a blend of investments in stocks, bonds, cash, and REIT funds ended up with respectable (though not stellar) returns.

Unfortunately, I cannot foretell the future and neither can you. Since the only certainty about the future is uncertainty, hedging your bets by diversifying across a variety of asset classes is one of the best strategies for optimizing your results. So how might you go about selecting an asset allocation that is appropriate for you? Let's start with the easiest solution.

The Default Option

The default option refers to "Target Date" funds offered by many mutual fund companies. If your employer offers a retirement plan like a 401(k), they may "default" you into one of these funds if you don't make an alternate investment choice. The investor selects a fund that reflects a date nearest to which he or she plans to retire. So, if you plan to retire in 2050, you would simply select the "Target Retirement 2050" fund.

When you're young, the management company weights the fund's investments toward the riskier asset classes with the hope of maximizing your return over time. Of course, those investments will also be more volatile and have a greater risk of short-term loss. As you get older, the fund's holdings are gradually adjusted to move an ever-greater proportion of the portfolio into assets perceived as more conservative as you approach retirement.

Using the Vanguard funds as an example once again, the Target Retirement 2010 fund has roughly 50% of its assets invested in stocks. The other 50% is in bonds. In contrast, the Target Retirement 2050 fund is 90% in stocks and 10% in bonds. The logic is that younger investors can afford to take more risk (and potentially receive a higher return) because they have more time to make up any short-term stock market losses. Older investors, on the other hand, generally want to take less risk because they wouldn't have as much time to rebuild a shattered portfolio if the market has a meltdown right before they retire.

If you look at the funds' disclosures, you'll see that the stock portfolios generally have a mix of domestic and international holdings. They are well diversified by using broad-based index funds. Similarly, the bond portfolios in these particular funds include quite an extensive mix of the bond market.

Sounds simple, right? Just set it and forget it. Conceptually, these funds are a great idea and work well for many. Of course, there are a few caveats. It turns out not all Target Date funds are created equal. During the great stock market meltdown of 2008 and early 2009, some mutual fund companies had a lot of explaining to do. Many Target Date funds for soon-to-be retirees suffered rather dramatic losses. Some investors close to retirement found out their funds were not invested in holdings that were as conservative as they thought. (Once again, I refer you back to Chapter 2, Principle #5, *"Pay Attention."*)

The other issue is that Target Date funds may not reflect your individual risk profile. For example, as a Vanguard 2050 fund investor, would you be comfortable having 90% of your assets being invested in stocks when you are age 25? For myself, I'd say, "probably yes." Would you be comfortable as a 65-year old having 50% of your assets in stocks as does the Vanguard 2010 target fund? For me personally, if I were that that age, I might want a bit less risk. (Yet, if I knew for sure I'd live to age 95, I might feel differently.)

However, I am not you. You need to read the disclosures that come with the fund, and decide what makes you comfortable.

If the mix of assets in a Target Date fund doesn't fit your preferences, you are not necessarily out of luck. For example, if you are age 25 and are not comfortable with such a high exposure to stocks, you might consider selecting a Target Date fund with an earlier retirement date. A Target 2030 fund would be invested more conservatively than a Target 2050, for example. This would reduce your exposure to riskier assets. (Don't forget that these funds invest even more conservatively as time goes on.)

Remember that the composition of the fund is not your only concern. You also have to pay attention to fees and expenses. As we saw earlier, small differences in a fund's expense ratio add up to a lot of money over several decades. Why give that money to Wall Street when it can stay in your pocket? If you are participating in an employer plan like a 401(k), you will not have a choice. You'll have to select from one of the options they present to you. You can only hope your employer has chosen wisely. An IRA account that you are managing on your own is different. Shop around. Find similar funds from a variety of firms, and then compare expense ratios.

Build Your Own Custom Portfolio

If you are a member of the do-it-yourself crowd, you could construct a portfolio on your own. By choosing to do this, it presupposes that:
- You have done your homework.
- You understand the asset classes you are proposing to invest in.
- You understand your risk profile.

- You are willing to monitor your investments.
- You are okay with the possibility of making a dumb mistake that will cost you some money.

Believe me, I have made my fair share of stupid decisions that in retrospect I wish I could take back. Unfortunately, hindsight doesn't count! As long as you invest in low-cost funds that are well diversified across a variety of asset classes, the odds are good that a mistake will not have a serious impact on your results.

Since you've chosen not to invest in one of the Target Date funds and are building your own portfolio from scratch, be sure you understand why. For example:

- Perhaps the Target Date funds are missing an asset class that you think would be helpful to you, such as real estate (REIT funds) or inflation-protected bonds.
- Maybe you are not finding a Target Date fund that has an investment mix that maps to your risk tolerance and time horizon.
- You just know you are the type of person who prefers to do it yourself. (Hmm. Is this a good reason? Just asking.)

A good place to start is to look at a variety of Target Date funds from several companies and see what is in them. You'll notice that most invest in a broad mix of bonds and stocks (both domestic and international). Carefully note the percentage allocated to each type of investment.

An old rule of thumb suggests that an appropriate proportion of stocks would be 100 minus your age. So, if you are 25 years old, this formula would suggest 100-25=75% recommended for stocks, the rest for bonds. For a 65-year old, the formula would be 100-65=35% in stocks. Use this rule (generally considered conservative) as a starting point and adjust it according to your risk tolerance.

Once you've arrived at an appropriate overall mix for stocks and bonds, the tricky part is allocating your money across the investing landscape. Assuming that you are sticking to low-cost index funds, here is a template that may help:

Bonds	Desired Allocation (%)
• Short-term bond funds	
• Intermediate-term bond funds	
• Inflation-protected bond funds	
• Long-term bond funds	
Bonds subtotal	
Stocks	
• Domestic stock funds	
• Real Estate Investment Trusts (REITs)	
• International (developed countries) stock funds	
• Emerging economies stock funds	
Stocks subtotal	
Grand total	100%

Making Your Choices

To fill in this table, first enter the percentage you've decided is appropriate for your overall mix of stocks and bonds. So, for example, if you want 70% of your money to go to stocks and 30% to bonds, then you would enter 30% under bonds subtotal and 70% under stocks subtotal.

Next, fill in the blanks for your specific investment choices under the stocks and bonds headings. Continuing with this example, if you wanted 30% to go to bonds, then the percentages you allocate to short, medium, long, and inflation-protected bond funds need to sum to 30%. Similarly, the lines under the stock heading would sum to 70%. For a guidepost, take a look at a variety of the lifecycle funds to see where they recommend cash be allocated for someone your age.

Here are some of the things you need to think about as you prepare to fill in the template:

- What percentage will you allocate to domestic versus foreign stocks? Do not neglect international investments, as significant growth occurs in economies outside the United States.
  - Remember that your return can be affected either positively or negatively, depending on changes in the exchange rates between the dollar and the foreign currency. (Refer back to the last chapter on stocks if you need a refresher.)
  - Within the international stock category, what proportion will go to countries with developed economies versus emerging economies? Or do you want to simplify your choices and just select an international index fund that includes a market-weighted mix of all international stocks?

- Inside the universe of domestic stocks, how will you distribute your money across the large, medium, and small stock funds? Will you simply buy a total domestic stocks index?
- For bonds, what will be your mix of short, medium, and long-term bond funds? Do you want to include inflation-protected bonds?

However you decide to construct your portfolio, just be sure you have thought about it and can make a good case as to why you approached your investments as you did. By choosing to construct your own mix of funds, presumably you had a pretty good reason. Be sure that each decision you make is well grounded with a good intellectual thought process behind it. If you are just throwing darts, you are gambling. That is not good!

What if you end up with an investment mix that is wildly different than a typical Target Date fund for someone your age? Be aware that a deviation that large may mean that you are assuming a level of risk that is excessive or is so conservative that your investment return will not satisfy your financial goals.

Rebalancing

If you have chosen to build your own custom portfolio, you will want to review your holdings once or twice a year to see whether the proportion you have allocated to each investment has significantly deviated from your desired mix. This can happen for a variety of reasons. One investment class might have had a huge gain and another might have done nothing or perhaps had a loss. Your carefully defined mix could then be out of whack.

For example, let's say you decided to allocate 60% of your money to stocks and 40% to bonds. Assume that over the past year, the stocks in your portfolio had a wonderful 30% gain and your bonds were unchanged in value. The proportion of stocks in your portfolio has now risen to 66% and the bond portion has dropped to 34% of the total portfolio value. Presuming that you still want a 60/40 mix of stocks to bonds, what should you do?

In a tax-advantaged account like an IRA or 401(k), it is easy to fix this. Once or twice a year, just reallocate the money with your account custodian or broker. Depending on the capabilities of your management company, you can simply tell them to reallocate to your desired mix. Alternately, you may need to sell a portion of the portfolio that has grown and buy more shares of the asset classes that have underperformed. You get the idea.

If your holdings are in a taxable account, rebalancing is a bit trickier. Selling anything with a gain in a non-retirement account will be a taxable event for the IRS. You can potentially avoid this by simply directing new money to the asset class that has been underperforming and suspend new investments in the over-performing areas until you get back to the mix you want.

Note that if your investments are in a Target Date fund, you will not have to worry about rebalancing. The management company will automatically keep an appropriate mix in each asset class according to the rules they have for that particular fund.

Market Timing and Dollar Cost Averaging

You've heard the phrase, "Buy low, sell high." It refers, of course, to an investor's desire to try to time the market to buy after a market correction (prices lower) and sell when prices get to a point where they seem overly pricey. This is wonderful in theory. In practice, it is difficult or impossible, especially for novices (and often for experts).

I once had a physician friend who was notorious for his lousy stock market timing—always buying and selling at the wrong times. He was after short-term profits and not investing for the long-term. After a while he concluded, "I buy no stock before its peak!" The rest of us decided that we should probably do the opposite of whatever our doctor friend was doing. (My brother the corporate treasurer says the best way to ensure that a stock drops is to buy it.)

Don't try to time the market. I have tried, with decidedly mixed results. I consider myself lucky to have moved a large portion of our investments out of the stock market in 2000 and 2007 when I feared that huge bubbles were building in equities (2000) and housing (2007). My concern both times was that prices of those assets had risen far above historical averages. I was happy to have avoided some nasty losses. The bad news is that I was too cautious about getting back in and missed some monster rallies that occurred after confidence returned to the market.

Bubbles like those that popped in 2000 and 2007 generally take a very long time to build. If you are nervous about a bubble forming, it is probably better to simply rebalance a bit more often than trying to chase performance by moving your money in and out of the market.

Dollar cost averaging is a much better way to get the best average price per share when you are buying an investment. The idea is that you invest a fixed amount of money at regular intervals (say monthly) regardless of market performance. When the market is in an uptrend, you are buying fewer shares each month than the prior month. When the market is falling, you end up with more shares. Employer-sponsored retirement plans like a 401(k) facilitate this type of purchasing. You simply have your employer withhold a fixed amount of money from your paycheck and they will forward it to the management company at defined intervals for investment purchases on your behalf.

You can easily do something similar with self-directed IRAs and your taxable investment accounts. Be sure to take into account any brokerage fees that may apply. Many mutual fund companies will allow regular purchases without a commission. Your broker may or may not, depending on the asset you are buying and the brokerage firm's commission schedule.

Do You Need Professional Help?

I'm not talking about psychotherapy. That book is in a different section of the library. No, I'm referring to seeking the assistance of a financial professional if all this feels overwhelming or if you don't know where to start. For those who are confident in what they are doing, finding a discount broker or going directly to the management company of the mutual funds they wish to buy is an easy choice. These companies offer a wealth of information on their websites for investors who prefer to do it themselves.

After reading through these chapters on investing, if you still feel intimidated or want to discuss your ideas with a financial professional before acting, then by all means do it! In my opinion, you are showing self-knowledge and confidence if you choose to seek the opinion of someone more knowledgeable than yourself.

When looking for professional advice, be cautious whom you select. Remember that you are a guppy swimming with sharks. I have had many friends ask me to informally review their brokerage statements and give my opinion of the investments their professional advisor has selected for them. On more occasions than I would have liked, I found funds with shockingly high sales loads and high expense ratios. Even worse, many of these investments were significantly underperforming their benchmark. These funds appeared to be selected to improve the paycheck of the broker, not to optimize the return for the client.

I've seen this sort of thing enough to develop a wonderful fantasy of what I'd like to do the next time a friend shows me a brokerage statement like that. My fantasy is to accompany my friend to the advisor's office and wait until the person takes a big gulp of their favorite beverage (milk would be ideal). In mid-gulp, I'd want to ask him or her if they'd be willing to fully refund their commission and fees if the investments they recommend (net of fees) reliably underperform their benchmark over a reasonable period of time. My goal is to see if I can time my question such that the milk squirts out their nose. You can try it, too. Let me know if you ever pull this off.

There are many smart, ethical people who are truly in business to help their clients become financially successful. There are several things you can do to enhance your odds of finding one:

- Ask several friends for a referral. If you find a number of people who have had a good experience with a particular advisor, consider that a good sign. However, take the referral as just a start in your investigation. Just because they seem to be a nice person does not necessarily mean they are competent or ethical.
- By law, brokers and financial advisors must be licensed and registered. Do some research to make sure the person you are considering has the necessary credentials. Dig further to determine whether regulators or a professional association has ever disciplined the advisor. Information on how to do this is available at **www.sec.gov/investor/brokers.htm**. You should also contact the advisor's professional association to verify that the person is a member in good standing.
- When you meet with the advisor for an informational session, ask how the individual is compensated. You want to make sure their interests are aligned with yours. If the person's paycheck is dependent on commissions they make by selling you a particular investment, you should assess whether you are comfortable with that type of compensation scheme. The risk for you is that the advisor's objectivity may be clouded.
- Be wary of: (1) anything that sounds too good to be true; (2) investments pitched as "can't lose!" or "guaranteed huge returns!"; and (3) comments that make you feel pressured to decide something immediately. Statements like that are good clues that you should bail out while you still have your cash in hand.

Before you make a commitment with an advisor, you should also be thinking about the following:

- Be clear what you want the advisor to do. Is your interest mainly in getting help developing a long-term financial plan and then you would take responsibility for executing it? Do you want to pay the advisor to select and manage investments on your behalf? Perhaps both?
- If you want your advisor to select and manage investments for you, it's a good idea to jointly develop some performance measurement criteria so you can see how your advisor's recommendations are performing against an objective benchmark. After all, if you're paying someone who is supposed to be better than you at this game, you would expect that the results would be at least as good as a market-neutral index, right? Remember to factor in fees when comparing results against your benchmark. Agree in advance to review performance at regular intervals.

- Be sure you understand any documents you are asked to sign. Don't feel pressured to sign anything immediately. Be sure the documents reflect the agreements you have made with the advisor, including fee schedules, what you have authorized (or not authorized) the advisor to do on your behalf, and how the agreement may be terminated if you want to end the relationship.

If I were looking for an advisor, I'd be looking for someone whose compensation is "fee only", meaning that they would charge me a flat amount for a particular service provided or a fixed percentage of the assets they are managing on my behalf. That way, I would feel more confident that the recommendations being made are objective. I personally would be cautious about working with someone who makes his or her money through commission-based selling. I'm not denigrating someone who earns his or her living in this way. I'm just saying that approach to compensation doesn't work for me because I could never be sure about someone's objectivity.

There are several professional designations for financial planners and advisors. Among the most comprehensive programs I have seen are the Certified Financial Planner (CFP®) and the Certified Public Accountant (CPA) with an added Personal Financial Specialist credential. What I find attractive about these programs is they have extensive education and experience requirements, together with robust professional ethics codes. Those who have gone to the trouble to make their way through all these requirements have, at a minimum, shown deep commitment to the profession. That said, be aware that a professional certification doesn't guarantee that a particular individual is necessarily a great advisor for you. Do your due diligence.

"And in Conclusion, Ladies and Gentlemen ..."

Okay, we're almost done! For those of you who drifted off to fantasyland from time to time, here is a quick thumbnail sketch of what you might have missed. In the last several chapters on investing, we covered the following topics:

- We reviewed the major investment classes, what they are, and how they work. In particular, we've completed a fairly detailed walkthrough on stocks and bonds, which are the essential components of a well-diversified portfolio.
- We discussed why it is important to understand your risk tolerance, as that will guide your selection of appropriate investments.

- We took a look at the difference between mutual funds and Exchange Traded Funds (ETFs) and examined why these are probably more appropriate choices for a novice investor as compared to buying individual stocks and bonds. We dug into the various fees that might be associated with these investments and did the math on why it is so important to focus on funds that have low expense ratios.
- We reviewed ways you might approach selecting your investments, maintaining an appropriate balance over time, and using dollar cost averaging.
- Finally, for those looking for help from a professional, we talked about some tips for finding a good financial advisor.

We covered a lot of material the last few chapters. Don't worry if it didn't all sink in the first time—it didn't for me either. I'd encourage you to reread any portions that you did not "get" right away. Understand, too, that this material is just an introductory overview. (Refer back to Principle #8 in Chapter 2, "*Continuously educate yourself.*") I strongly encourage you to read everything you can about investing so that you will continue to improve your skills and decision-making in this area throughout your lifetime. My website will point you to other references that you may find of value.

After my epiphany with the mortgage banker at age 25, I got my spending under control. Those actions let me pay off my credit cards and begin to accumulate lots of cash. However, it was investing that turbo-charged the growth of my money, especially during the go-go years of the 1990s. There is no way my financial position would be as good as it is now had I not learned how to invest and, more importantly, had I not jumped into the game. There are few things as exciting as comparing your brokerage statements at year-end to the statements from years past to see the amazing growth in your cash over time. If you make the effort now, my bet is that you will be well rewarded over the long term.

Getting Into Action

> *"Always bear in mind that your own resolution to succeed is more important than any other one thing."*
> — ABRAHAM LINCOLN

CHAPTER 13

What's Your Magic Number?

"A large income is the best recipe for happiness I ever heard of."
— JANE AUSTEN

In this chapter, we'll talk about how much money you will need to accumulate to live the life you want to live in retirement (or when you're ready to live off your investments rather than depending on a corporate job).

I can hear some of you saying, "Are you kidding? I am 21-years-old and just started my first job. I can only afford ramen noodles for dinner, and you're asking me to think about retirement?" Yes, I am, and here's why.

We have now come full circle. This book started with a story about me being a financially clueless 25-year old attempting to get my first mortgage loan while having a net worth of $500. I suspect many of you are now in the same position I was those 25 years ago. Perhaps you are not as financially clueless as I was then, but you are just beginning to build an independent financial life and are looking forward to the many adventures life will bring. Student loans may be weighing on you. You want to have some fun now that you're on your own, but you don't have all the money you need (or want). All the money you have seems to be gone before you know it. Believe me, I've been there and I know how it feels.

So why do I urge you to deal with this now, in your 20s? Think back to the Life Vision you wrote back in Chapter 3. How many of the dreams and goals in that Life Vision will require a fair amount of cash to make them real? Do you want to buy a house eventually? Have kids? Help them pay for college? Travel? Do you want to ditch your corporate job in your 40s or 50s and be free to pursue anything you want? In mid-life and beyond, do you want to live a life that is free of financial worries—where you know you will have the money to do what you want?

Unless you were our lucky trust fund baby in the Uncle Sam chapter, the only way that money is going to show up is if you make it happen. Look around you, especially at the people you know who are in mid-life and beyond. Are they happy with where they are financially and are they able to do the things they want? If you have a strong relationship with them, ask them what they did to get there. What about the older people you know who clearly are struggling with money? What can you learn from them? Consider asking them what they wish they had done differently.

With a little bit of effort now, in your 20s, you can set yourself on a path to financial liberation. And here's the thing. Though you may be somewhat cash poor, you are time rich. Unlike your parents and grandparents, you have many decades ahead of you. That means you don't need to save very much, comparatively speaking, if you get going now. (I can hear you now: "Yeah, yeah, I know. $4.25 per day starting at age 21 invested at an average 8% annual return in the stock market will get me $1 million in 50 years. Don't tell me that again. I got it.")

When you are driving on a deserted country road on a long trip, aren't you glad to have headlights to take a peek at what's ahead? In this chapter, I want to give you headlights for future numbers so that you will have a better chance at knowing what is coming at you financially. That way, you'll be able to prepare well in advance and make the appropriate adjustments so that you don't run off the road later on your financial journey.

How Much Will You Need to Live Off Your Investments?

How much will you need to be financially independent and live off your investments, whether in your 40s or 70s? There is no easy answer to that question, as many variables are involved. Expert opinion seems divided on the answer. However, we can derive some rough approximations to get you started.

My two smarty-pants answers to the "How much will I need?" question are: (1) "Probably more than you think"; and (2) "It depends." The variables you will need to think about include:

- **What is your life expectancy?** Someone born in 1990 could live well into their early 90s or beyond if they have good genes and a healthy lifestyle.
- **At what age would you like to retire?** Clearly, the more years you are working, the shorter the time period you'll need to rely on your investments to support you. If your Life Vision calls for being done with a corporate job in your late 40s, your investments may need to support you for 50 years unless you have another source of income. Even if you don't retire until age 65, your money may need to last 25-30 years beyond that.
- **What is the likelihood that Social Security and Medicare will be able to provide benefits that are currently promised?** Both programs are currently on the path to insolvency. The government will have a diffi-cult time paying the benefits promised without major changes in the way they operate. The obvious choices are to: (1) push out the official retirement age; (2) cut benefits; (3) increase taxes to pay the benefits;

or (4) some combination of these. You can make your own guess as to the likely outcome. It is unlikely we will avoid all four of these courses of action. How much do you want to depend on the benefits, as they currently exist, to be there when you need them?

- **How high will your health care expenses be when your older?** Health care costs are rising well above the general rate of inflation. As you get older, you will likely consume many more medical services than you do now. If you Google the phrase "Estimating health care costs in retirement" you'll find studies that suggest the average 65-year-old couple will spend over $200,000 in health care (2010 dollars) during their retirement years.

- **Do you want to leave anything to your kids or do you want to spend it all?** You're on your own with this decision, but it should factor into your thinking.

- **How much risk are you willing to take with your investments?** Remember, $4.25 per day invested in stocks (at 8%) yields over $800,000 more in 50 years than in CDs (at 3%). If you wanted to amass $1,000,000 from bank CDs you would need to increase your contributions from $125 per month to about $725 per month! Where do you fall on the risk/reward spectrum? I'm not suggesting a path of all stocks or all bank CDs. On the contrary, you will need a blend of stocks, bonds, and cash to be adequately diversified and have an acceptable level of risk. What you need to consider is the proportion of your assets that will be allocated to riskier asset classes as compared to more conservative investments.

- **Will you spend more or less money in your retirement than you did while working?** This is good topic to Google if you want to study the debate. Some advisors suggest you'll need about 75% of your pre-retirement income. Others say much more. Do you want to travel more in retirement? Spend more on entertainment? Are you living a lifestyle now that will likely mean higher than average medical expenses when you're older? All these questions (and more) factor into this.

- **Will your mortgage be paid off by the time you exit the workforce?** As you probably could surmise by now, I think carrying zero debt into retirement is a good thing. Having the mortgage disappear significantly reduces monthly cash needs. The last thing I'd want as a 65-year-old is to still be writing mortgage checks to my bank every month. Ugh.

I realize it's asking a lot to think about these questions when you are at the beginning of your working life. You do not need to know all the answers right now. I can assure you that when you get to your 40s and beyond, these questions become more vivid and relevant. The reason you need to ponder these questions right now is that you have the benefit of time on your side. As we've discussed earlier, that time works in your favor if you act on it.

My intent here is to get you thinking about taking steps now that will enable you to be responsible for your own financial independence once you leave the workforce, whether that is in your 40s, 60s, or beyond. The last thing you want is to be broke (or nearly so) in retirement and totally dependent on whatever government aid programs may or may not be available. Time will not be on your side for very long. Let's take a look at how you might estimate how much you will need.

What's Your Magic Number?

So what is the "magic number" you'd need to have in your investment accounts to consider yourself financially independent? Let's walk through some rules of thumb that might help you arrive at a rough estimate. For purposes of simplicity, let's assume that you are currently 21 years old and that you'll retire at age 65. You have good genes and a healthy lifestyle, so we'll presume that you will live into your early 90s. We will ignore any Social Security payments you may receive. We'll also ignore all the other variables mentioned earlier that might influence your cash needs—you'll have to factor those in on your own.

Use the Rule of 72 to Estimate Inflation's Impact

Let's start by bringing the Rule of 72 back into the discussion. Remember that this formula helps us estimate how long it will take for a given number to double when we apply a particular interest rate. Take 72 and divide it into the interest rate to get the answer (72/interest rate = years to double).

Let's use this formula to estimate what your monthly cash needs might be at retirement compared to now. We'll assume that you are age 21 and spend $2,000 per month. Further, you expect to have about the same monthly outlay once you reach age 65, but in inflation-adjusted dollars. Finally, we'll assume that inflation will average 3% per year from age 21 to age 65.

Applying the Rule of 72, if you are spending $2,000 at age 21, it will double to $4,000 when you turn 45 in 24 years. (Here's the calculation: 72/3=24 years. Age 21+24=45.) In 24 more years, it will double again to $8,000/month at age 69. See how damaging inflation can be? At age 69, the inflation-adjusted number is four times higher than age 21. Assuming the relative cost of the goods and services you're consuming remains constant, you'll spend four times as much to maintain the lifestyle you had at age 21!

Remember that the Rule of 72 just gives an approximation. To derive the exact number, I used a financial calculator and came up with $8,426 per month rather than the $8,000 estimate given by the Rule of 72. Close enough for our purposes, but you can see the limitation of the estimating formula.

Calculating the Magic Number

We said you wanted to retire at age 65, not 69. If you didn't have a financial calculator, you could fudge a bit and nudge the $8,000 down to, let's say, $7,500. (The financial calculator gives you exactly $7,475 if you're wondering.)

Now let's estimate how large your savings would need to be to support spending $7,500 per month at age 65. I have read a lot on this and have yet to find a firm professional consensus about the rate you can withdraw to ensure that you won't run out of money. (You can Google this topic to read more on your own.)

That said, there does seem to be a general rule of thumb. A 4% withdrawal rate in year one of retirement at age 65 is a pretty good approximation if you assume a moderate rate of return on your investment portfolio after that age.

In our current example, to withdraw $7,500 per month, you would multiply by 12 to calculate the annual withdrawal ($7,500 x 12 = $90,000), and then by 25 to arrive at the "magic number" which is $2,250,000 ($90,000 x 25). So, the balance in your investment and saving accounts would need to be $2,250,000 to support your retirement at age 65.

Are you shocked at the size of the number? I want the answer to have a dramatic effect—and inspire you to start putting money away NOW. At the same time, I don't want you to look at the size of the number and get discouraged.

Don't Depend on This Number—It's Just a Start

The calculation we just performed is quite oversimplified and ignores all the other variables that might affect your actual financial requirements in retirement. While the math calculations are reasonably accurate, the underlying assumptions may or may not be. We did not consider any of the life events you may experience, such as marriage, having children, paying for kids' college, buying a house, and acquiring other material possessions. These events will have an impact on your current expenses and your ability to save. Some of these expenses will permanently increase your cash needs. Others may drop off before retirement, thereby reducing your cash needs. With that in mind, here are some other things to ponder that might alleviate the sticker shock:

- We did not include Social Security payments in this example. With luck, Uncle Sam will make the system solvent so that your generation can at least depend somewhat on it.
- Our example was based on a 21-year-old who is spending $2,000 per month. This may not even vaguely approximate your situation. You should assess how your spending habits are likely to change as you move through life. As you get older you'll be able to do this with more precision. For now, you should at least take a shot at it to have something to work with.
- We assumed you'd be spending roughly the same amount at age 65 as you were at 21. The number might be significantly lower or higher, depending on your plans.
- With discipline, your mortgage can be paid off by age 65. This could significantly decrease your housing expense. You may also downsize to a smaller property and be able to extract some house equity for your retirement.
- Remember that $125 per month invested at 8% for 50 years will generate about one million dollars. You'd have twice that amount if you set aside $250 per month.
- Your salary will likely increase throughout your working years making it easier to save ever-larger amounts each month. (This presumes, of course, that you don't ramp up your spending proportionately.)

Taking the Shortcut

Is this feeling overwhelming? While I strongly encourage you to try the "magic number" exercise, I also get that there's a lot of math involved, and that the time horizon is so far into the future that it might be difficult for you to get your head around doing it.

If this is the case, let me offer a short-term short cut. At a minimum, you should be saving at least 10% of your gross income. Every time you get a raise at work, direct at least half to your savings and investment accounts. These actions will at least set you on the right path. A few years from now, take another try at these calculations, with the help of a financial professional if necessary.

Other Scenarios

What if you want to retire before you are 65? What if you have a goal to be financially independent in your 50s or even your 40s? What if you want to change around a bunch of other variables to see how that would affect your magic number? The rough estimates we did earlier are not as helpful with these questions.

There are other options to consider to help you get answers. The first is to talk to a financial professional like a Certified Financial Planner®. They have fairly sophisticated computer models that can more accurately approximate your situation.

Another option is to try several free web-based retirement calculators. Most investment management companies provide such tools. Just Google the topic and you will find dozens of them. For those of you looking to satisfy your inner geek, the HP12C is the granddaddy of financial calculators. I've had mine since 1982 and it has seen a great deal of use. You can model both simple and complex scenarios and have the answer quickly. Many large office supplies stores carry this and other financial calculators.

Revising the Number

Your magic number will not remain static throughout your life. The life events we talked about earlier and other changes in your spending patterns will affect your result. You should review your assumptions and calculations every so often to determine whether you need to make any changes.

In your 20s and 30s, it is not important to have a precise magic number as long as you are saving and investing an amount that will get you within range of your rough estimate. As you move into your early 40s, you should develop a number that is more precise, either on your own or with the help of a pro. Continue to refine this number and check your progress against it.

The last thing you want is to retire, find out you came up short, and have to go back to eating ramen noodles for dinner.

CHAPTER 14

Now What?

"Start by doing what's necessary; then do what's possible;
and suddenly you are doing the impossible."
— SAINT FRANCIS OF ASSISI

Now that you have all this knowledge about personal finance, what do you do with it? In this final chapter, I've prepared a summary of action items and things to review. The time you just spent reading this book will have no value unless you put the things you've learned into action. I hope to inspire you to do just that.

Please, Get into Action on Your Personal Finances–Now!

Think back to the Japanese proverb from Chapter 3–"Vision without action is a daydream. Action without vision is a nightmare."

After making your way through this book, you should have a pretty good idea of the role you want money to play in your life. We've covered the details of managing, saving, and investing your money. You have the tools at your disposal. They will do you no good unless you start using them.

I would like to make a request. As soon as you put down this book, please jot down at least three things that you will put into action. Tell three friends what you're going to do and ask them to hold you accountable. Request they check in with you in three months to see whether you have completed the things you said you would do. After those three months, repeat the process. Making a public commitment to people you care about will help cement the commitments you have made to yourself. Without resolving to take concrete steps to advance your financial life, odds are that all the other things in your busy life will take over and nothing will change.

In the last few hundred pages, I've tried to share everything I've learned about managing my money the last 25 years. After all that time, I still don't consider myself an expert. There's so much to learn! This book hasn't covered everything you'd see if you were studying to be a financial professional. However, I believe it has covered enough to give you a really good start.

Don't let this book be the end of your financial education. Make a commitment to yourself to subscribe to financial periodicals and read books from well-regarded authors to continue developing your financial skills. My website has some suggested resources that you might consider.

Giving Back

This book has mostly focused on how to manage, save, and invest money. I did not want to end a discussion on personal finance without saying something about giving back to causes that have meaning for you. At some point, sooner or later, you will likely think about this, especially as your wealth grows. Some of you may already be giving generously, despite being early in your career and possibly having limited financial assets. Either way, I want to encourage you to give some consideration to this.

In general, I would respectfully suggest that you "put your own oxygen mask on first" when considering the level of financial generosity you wish to pursue. By that I mean be sure that your own financial house is in order and that charitable giving is a part of your overall financial planning and budgeting processes. If you have significant debt, there may be other ways to contribute to the well being of others without making your own financial situation worse. For example, you could contribute your time by volunteering at a community service agency that tugs at your heartstrings.

I want to respect whatever spiritual or religious beliefs you may have. If those beliefs require a certain level of financial giving, by all means honor those beliefs. Just be sure that you have explicitly planned for those expenses in your budget.

You may find that Uncle Sam can be very helpful in supporting your generosity. IRS Form 526 ("*Charitable Contributions*") describes the circumstances under which you may derive tax benefits from your gifts to charitable organizations.

Ten Clues You're a "Financial Grownup"

Many people have never developed the money management skills that will enable them to live a life free of financial worry. This became abundantly clear during the housing and financial crisis of 2008-2009. Millions of people lost their homes to foreclosure. Some had this happen due to circumstances truly beyond their control. The vast majority, however, likely ended up in trouble because they did not have the financial skills to clearly understand the risks they were taking.

How will you know whether you have developed sufficient skills to consider yourself a "financial grownup"? By that I mean you have learned and applied skills in saving, managing, and investing your money to truly operate independently without dragging a lot of debt and other financial baggage around behind you. Here's my attempt at identifying a set of clues that might help you decide whether you have arrived at financial maturity or not:

1. You reliably save and invest at least 10% of your gross income.
2. You never pay full retail price on your purchases.
3. You only use credit cards for convenience and pay them in full every month.
4. You have no debt, except a reasonably-sized mortgage and perhaps some student loans.
5. Money is not a constant source of stress and anxiety.
6. Your housing expenses are what you can reasonably afford without stretching yourself too much financially. If you own a house, you think of it as a place to live first and an investment second.
7. You have taken care of the paperwork that documents how you want things to be handled if you become incapacitated or die.
8. You're giving back to causes that are meaningful to you and make a difference in the world.
9. You are constantly educating yourself about changes in the financial world and how to play the game even better.
10. Bonus points: You can't wait to read *The Wall Street Journal* every morning and you know how to use a financial calculator.

A Summary Checklist of Action Items and Things to Review

The checklist that follows is organized by chapter. That way, you can go back and refer to the relevant text if you need a refresher. You do not need to do the items in sequential order. However, I have tried to organize the checklist such that it would make sense to first deal with the items listed earliest, then to tackle the ones at the end later on. If you would prefer a different approach, do what works best for you. I recommend you check off each item when it is complete and when you are certain you understand the educational material behind it. Know that completing this list will take a while. Focus on making steady progress.

The Big Picture (Chapters 1, 2, and 3)

☐ Think about what you learned about money from your parents and from school. What works for you? What doesn't? What do you want to change? What do you want to know that you don't? What might be standing in the way of achieving your financial goals?

☐ Identify the good financial habits you would like to keep. Separately list the bad habits you would like to get rid of. Develop a plan to do so.

- [ ] Construct a Life Vision statement to get clarity on what you want from life and establish the role that money will play.
- [ ] Understand the time value of money and compound interest. Be clear on why investing a relatively small amount of savings early in life can make a huge difference to your financial well being later on.
- [ ] Develop a plan for using "good" debt sparingly. Commit to avoiding all "bad" debt.
- [ ] Create a list of expenses comprising your essential "needs" for living independently. Clearly distinguish between the essentials and everything else.
- [ ] Resolve to always pay less than full retail price on everything you buy! To get started, choose three things you usually pay full price for and find a cheaper way to obtain them. After you succeed, choose three more. Repeat until you are certain you are paying the lowest possible price in every transaction.
- [ ] Understand your risk tolerance so that you can make appropriate investment decisions. Be clear where you stand on the risk/reward scale so that you can sleep well, yet still achieve your long-term financial goals. Write down a simple summary describing your risk tolerance. Refer to it when needed.
- [ ] Identify the next set of resources that you will use to continue your financial education. These might include books, periodicals, and financial education courses from reputable providers. My website has some ideas for you.
- [ ] Ensure that your approach to personal finance feels uplifting and full of possibility and abundance. If it's not feeling like fun, figure out why not and try a different approach.

Getting Started (Chapter 4)

- [ ] Understand your credit score.
- [ ] Check your credit files annually and correct any inaccuracies.
- [ ] Take steps to prevent identity theft.
- [ ] Develop a budget. Review actual versus estimated expenses monthly.
- [ ] Open a no-fee checking account with an ATM/debit card. Have your paycheck directly deposited to the checking account.
- [ ] Obtain a no-fee credit card that rebates cash. Read the fine print to make sure that miscellaneous charges will not negate the benefit of the cash rebate.
- [ ] Pay the credit card in full every month without exception.

☐ Open a savings account at a bank or credit union. Set up automatic deductions from your checking account to savings.

☐ Build an emergency fund of 3-6 months of living expenses and put it in an account that is insured by a government agency.

☐ Whenever you get a raise at work, change your automatic savings withholding to direct at least half of the salary increase to your savings or investment accounts.

☐ Determine the proper insurance coverage you will need. Solicit the recommendations of three or four good insurance agents. Comparison shop for quotes.

☐ Review all the benefits offered by your employer and take advantage of everything that is relevant to your situation. Don't pass up "free money" like 401(k) matches, etc.

☐ Set a date by which you will deal with all the paperwork that documents how you want things to be handled if you become incapacitated or die. Meet that deadline!

Uncle Sam (Chapter 5)

☐ Understand the difference between a progressive tax and a regressive tax. Make a list of the taxes you pay and determine in which category they reside. Do this so that you are clear on which taxes are influenced by how much money you make and which ones are not.

☐ Each year, determine your federal (and state, if applicable) marginal income tax rate. Understand how that rate may affect your decisions on various tax deductions like mortgage interest, property taxes, charitable donations, and so on.

☐ Understand how stock dividend and stock sale taxation is different from wage income taxation. Know the difference between a short and long-term capital gain. Apply this knowledge in your investment decisions.

☐ Fully internalize how a tax deduction and a tax credit differ.

☐ Review your paycheck to see how much is withheld for Social Security and Medicare. Visit **www.ssa.gov** (Social Security) and **www.medicare.gov** (Medicare) to learn more about these programs and why they will be important to you in the future.

☐ Review the list of tax-advantaged retirement plans supported by Uncle Sam. Know which ones might be available through your employer and which ones might be appropriate for you to manage on your own.

☐ Open and fund a retirement account after discussing with your tax pro and/or financial advisor, as appropriate.

- [ ] Do more research or consult with your financial professional to find other tax breaks that might be relevant to your situation.

Spending (Chapters 6, 7, and 8)

- [ ] Fund the necessities first. If money is left over, stick to your budget for the optional expenses.
- [ ] Reduce your monthly spending. Create a spreadsheet for each item that you will eliminate or acquire at a cheaper price. Calculate monthly and annual savings for each item and for the entire list in total. Prioritize them. Allocate half of the savings to your emergency fund or to your long-term investments.
- [ ] At every month end, review bank and credit card statements to see what expenses could be eliminated or reduced. Add these items to the above spreadsheet.
- [ ] Never pay full retail price on anything! Before buying, relentlessly review the price options or comparison shop to pay the least amount possible. Negotiate prices when appropriate. Be careful with impulse purchases.
- [ ] Clearly understand the impact (including opportunity cost) that a car has on your finances. Budget for maintenance, repairs, registration fees, gasoline, and insurance.
- [ ] Remember that a vehicle that gets twice the gas mileage will save you about 10% on your overall auto expense.
- [ ] If you purchase a home, think of it as a place to live, not an investment. Be careful about stretching for a place you cannot reasonably afford. The economic benefits become more compelling when the after-tax cost of owning is less than or equal to renting.
- [ ] Budget for insurance, property tax, maintenance, HOA fees, and other expenses that go along with home ownership.
- [ ] Avoid mortgages with negative amortization. Avoid second mortgages, Home Equity Lines of Credit (HELOCs), and other debt that lets you extract equity from your home.

Investing (Chapters 9, 10, and 11)

- [ ] Know how to use the Rule of 72 to get a rough idea of how long it will take a sum of money to double.
- [ ] Be able to explain what a bond is. Understand how you might lose money on a bond if you have to sell it during periods of rising interest rates or how you might make a profit if you sell during periods of falling interest rates.

From Ramen to Riches

Know the difference between investment grade and junk bonds.

☐ Be aware of the tax advantages that may exist for certain bonds issued by government entities. These include municipal bonds, U.S. Treasuries, and state government bonds.

☐ Be clear on how short, medium, and long-term bonds tend to differ in terms of interest rate payouts and volatility. Know where various types of bonds fall on the risk/reward scale.

☐ Be able to explain how stocks represent fractional ownership or equity in a company. Understand how stocks have tended to deliver good returns over the very long term, but with occasional (and lengthy) periods of significant underperformance and volatility. Know where stocks fall on the risk/reward scale.

☐ Be clear that past performance does not necessarily mean that an investment (or investment class) will continue that performance in the future.

☐ Review the role that stock dividends can play in the overall investment return and cash flow delivered to the investor.

☐ Understand how stock and bond mutual funds (and ETFs) work and why they might be a better choice for novice investors than buying individual securities.

☐ Be able to articulate how mutual funds and Exchange Traded Funds (ETFs) are similar and how they are different.

☐ Be sure you have internalized the concepts of asset allocation and diversification before you begin thinking about making any investment decisions.

☐ Review the list of common investment classes ranked from lowest risk (lower return) to higher risk (potentially higher return). Make investments that are compatible with your risk profile so that you can sleep well, yet still achieve your long-term financial goals.

☐ Create a filing system (paper or electronic) to keep track of paperwork for investment purchase and sales transactions. You will need to reference these at tax time, sometimes years later.

☐ Find investments with very low expense ratios to avoid the negative impact that high fees have on long-term returns.

Determining How Much You Need and Where to Put It (Chapters 12 and 13)

☐ Do a rough estimate of your "magic number"—the amount of money you will need to retire or to live off your savings. Figure out how much you need to save and invest to accumulate that amount.

☐ Decide the percentage of your assets that you want to allocate to each investment class. Your goal is to achieve adequate diversification, a sufficient investment return, and a level of risk that is in alignment with your risk tolerance. Evaluate Target Date funds to see if the asset allocation in those funds might meet your needs. If not, adjust accordingly.

☐ If you built a custom portfolio, rebalance investments once or twice a year to stay within the percentages you established in your asset allocation model. Be aware of tax implications if you rebalance in taxable accounts.

☐ Understand how dollar cost averaging works. Invest a fixed dollar amount at regular intervals to buy shares at the best average price. Avoid market timing.

☐ If you are uncomfortable investing on your own, seek help from a qualified financial professional. Do the necessary due diligence to find someone competent, qualified, ethical, and licensed. Understand the fees you will be paying. Make sure that any fees or commissions will not get in the way of an advisor's objectivity.

As you read through the checklist, be sure to review the relevant concepts in the chapters listed if you are not clear on what needs to be done. Don't feel like you need to tackle all these action items immediately. Remember that this is a life-long pursuit. At the same time, don't dawdle. Deal with as many as you can now and have a plan for when you will get back to the items that you set aside.

You Can Do This!

If you are in your early 20s, allocating less than $5 a day to your long-term investment account will make you a millionaire after 50 years, assuming an average 8% rate of return. That is less than a car payment. If you can afford a car, you can afford to do this to secure your financial future.

As we discussed earlier, many of you may need a lot more than $1,000,000 to retire comfortably, especially after including the impact of inflation. It will be far less stressful to start now than it will be in 10 or 20 years. As you now know, waiting to save until your 30s and beyond makes the job much, much tougher. I had someone tell me once that, "The days can be long, but the years go by fast." Now that I am in my early 50s, I can testify to the truth of that statement.

After an inauspicious start to my financial life, I am grateful that I started paying attention early enough to turn things around. The actions I took enabled me to retire from my corporate job at age 47, have a paid-off mortgage, and retirement account balances that will fund a decent retirement for my wife and me. I am grateful this has given me lots of time to spend with my son while he's still young enough to think that hanging out with Dad is cool. I am grateful to have time to be with my wife when most people are out working. I am grateful to have control of my time.

I do not know what you decided to write in your Life Vision and the role that you want money to play. My guess is that the absence of money would make many of the things on your list much more difficult to achieve. Live your dreams! Take command of your financial life to allow that to happen. Take the first steps today and keep building the "mental muscles" to make personal finance an automatic part of how you run your life. I wish you a great voyage as you dream your dreams and live a wonderful life.

Index

From Ramen to Riches

For updates and more resources,
please visit my website at:
www.fromramentoriches.com

Follow me on Twitter at:
www.twitter.com/fromramentorich

* * * * *

I have one last request for you. I hope this book will be a good resource for a long time to come. When you're finally done with it, please consider donating it to your local library or passing it on to a friend so that this information can reach as many people as possible. Thanks!

About The Author

The oldest of nine children, Jim Wood is a natural coach and mentor. His mission is to share his passion for personal finance by increasing financial literacy, especially for those aged 18 to 30 who can most benefit from this knowledge.

Jim retired from his corporate job at age 47 after 25 years in high tech. He held positions as a software engineer, information technology manager, and business strategy manager. He earned a bachelor's degree in Psychology with Distinction from Boston University. He also holds a master's degree in Engineering Management from Stanford University.

Jim lives in San Diego, California with his wife and son.

20372340R00111

Made in the USA
Lexington, KY
31 January 2013